Encountering the Poems
of Daisaku Ikeda

Encountering the Poems of Daisaku Ikeda

RONALD A. BOSCO
KENNETH M. PRICE
SARAH ANN WIDER

The Ikeda Center for Peace, Learning, and Dialogue
Cambridge, Massachusetts
2015

Published by the Ikeda Center for Peace, Learning, and Dialogue
396 Harvard Street
Cambridge, Massachusetts 02138

© 2015 by Ronald A. Bosco, Kenneth H. Price, Sarah Ann Wider
Original poems (in Japanese) © Daisaku Ikeda, 1945–2007
Translated poems (in English) © Soka Gakkai, 2014

All rights reserved
Printed in the United States of America

Cover design by Gopa & Ted2, Inc.
Interior design by Gopa & Ted2, Inc., and Eric Edstam

ISBN: 978-1-887917-13-1

Library of Congress Cataloging-in-Publication Data

Encountering the Poems of Daisaku Ikeda / Ronald A. Bosco, Kenneth M. Price, Sarah Ann Wider.
   pages cm
   Includes bibliographical references.
   ISBN 978-1-887917-13-1 (alk. paper)
1. Ikeda, Daisaku—Criticism and interpretation. 2. Japanese poetry—20th century—History and criticism. 3. Soka Gakkai Buddhists—Japan. 4. Buddhist philosophy in literature. 5. Comparative literature—American and Japanese. 6. Comparative literature—Japanese and American.
I. Bosco, Ronald A. II. Price, Kenneth M. III. Wider, Sarah Ann.
   PL853.K33Z59 2015
   895.61'5—dc23

                                                      2015007396

10 9 8 7 6 5 4 3 2 1

About the Ikeda Center

The Ikeda Center for Peace, Learning, and Dialogue is a not-for-profit institution founded by Buddhist thinker and leader Daisaku Ikeda in 1993. Located in Cambridge, Massachusetts, the Center engages diverse scholars, activists and social innovators in the search for the ideas and solutions that will assist in the peaceful evolution of humanity. Ikeda Center programs include public forums and scholarly seminars that are organized collaboratively and offer a range of perspectives on key issues in global ethics. The Center was initially called the Boston Research Center for the 21st Century and became the Ikeda Center in 2009.

For more information, visit the Ikeda Center website.
www.ikedacenter.org

Table of Contents

Introduction by Ronald A. Bosco   1

"A Wondrous Symphony of Life":
Lyricism in the Poems of Daisaku Ikeda   9
Ronald A. Bosco

A New Errand Bearer:
Daisaku Ikeda's Poetic Response to
Walt Whitman and His Quest for Peace   59
Kenneth M. Price

Daisaku Ikeda's Poetry of Encouragement   93
Sarah Ann Wider

About the Authors   161

About the Poet   163

Poems quoted in this volume are mainly taken from *Journey of Life: Selected Poems of Daisaku Ikeda*, published in 2014 by I.B. Tauris. Citations and poetry titles refer to *Journey of Life* unless otherwise stated.

Introduction

THE THREE WRITERS whose essays appear in *Encountering the Poems of Daisaku Ikeda* intend this volume, and their respective contributions to it, as a companion to *Journey of Life: Selected Poems of Daisaku Ikeda*, the first of a projected three-volume compilation of poems translated into English from the original Japanese.

Although the three authors, Ronald A. Bosco, Kenneth M. Price and Sarah Ann Wider, are professors of literature with, collectively, more than a century's worth of teaching experience in the university classroom, their individual approaches to and readings of Ikeda's poetry are neither prescriptive nor exhaustive. Rather, in the essays that follow, they each have undertaken to recount in prose their experience of reading, interpreting and personally—and independently—responding to various poems collected in *Journey of Life* in the spirit in which Ikeda has himself overseen the process wherein he chose poems for inclusion in the volume and placed the whole into production for publication.

Foremost to our own appreciation of the spirit in which Ikeda writes and shares his poems with a public that includes close friends, new acquaintances, students associated with the global Soka Gakkai community, heads of state and heroes of our time such as Corazon Aquino and Nelson Mandela, and authors and artists such as Nataliya Sats, Yehudi Menuhin, Oswald Mtshali and Esther Gress is the fact that for Ikeda there is no single "right" or "correct" reading of a poem. Ikeda understands and practices poetry much in the same way he understands the purpose of life and lives his own. Poetry, like life itself, is for Ikeda an ongoing series of pilgrimages: pilgrimages of the heart, pilgrimages of the imagination, pilgrimages of the intellect, pilgrimages of feeling in which people share the joys, succor the sorrows and advance the aspirations of all with whom they interact—pilgrimages, in sum, through which each and every one of us ultimately identifies ourselves as individuals within, as well as beneficiaries and benefactors of, a much larger community to which we belong: Humanity. Recognizing that the power of the human community lies in its ability to appreciate and celebrate its diversity, as a spiritual thinker and humanistic writer Ikeda thrives on the challenge always confronting the poet to "perceive the infinite possibilities of humanity" and transform that perception into poetry:

> I believe that if a poet can perceive the infinite possibilities of humanity, his poetry naturally becomes a song in praise of humanity. The perception of those possibilities is really the perception of interconnectedness, like that between friends, between humanity and nature, and between humanity and the cosmos. Poetry crystallizes the surprise and emotion of awakening to such connections.[1]

Ikeda's conception of what constitutes the poetic involves substantial work on the part of both poets and their readers. It is work that relies on poets' and readers' exercise of an inner spirit of open, selfless inquiry, a conviction of their relatedness to everyone and everything outside of themselves, and a willingness to share their thoughts, dreams, fears and hopes on behalf of humanity with all they encounter. Characterizing the seamless overlap between his work as a poet and his work as a champion for world peace, an advocate for the cessation of sectarian violence, a spokesman for the environment and an educator whose mission is solidly grounded in the value-creating spiritual life of Nichiren Buddhism, Ikeda has written,

> My daily life
> abounds with joys
> and my heart is never
> without employment.
> ("To my young friends," p. 28)

It is "employment" that admirably compensates the poet and the reader for their work.

Pilgrimages are often characterized as journeys to a specific place: perhaps to a site of spiritual significance for an individual such as Jerusalem, Mecca, Rome or Eagle Peak (Skt *Gridhrakūta*); perhaps to a monument that expresses humanity's creative genius across the ages such as Stonehenge in England or Hagia Sophia in Turkey or to one that transforms humanity's shame into an affirmation of the dignity of life for the sake of future generations such as the Hiroshima Peace Memorial in Japan; perhaps to one of the world's natural wonders such as Mount Everest or Mount Fuji, Australia's Great Barrier Reef, Africa's Victoria Falls or North America's Grand Canyon, the sheer majesty of which piques in the pilgrim-observer a resolve to protect and preserve the environment with which humanity was originally blessed.

No one undertakes a pilgrimage to such sites lightly; depending upon the site, a pilgrimage requires of the traveler seriousness of purpose and significant mental, physical and, possibly, spiritual preparation. Such journeys ask as much of a traveler as the poet does of himself and his readers; whether writing or reading a poem, one must willingly go wherever the heart, imagination, intellect and feeling take him. Without openness to our finer instincts, impressions and impulses, neither poets nor readers can avail themselves of the "surprise and emotion" of, literally, experiencing an "awakening" under the influence of poetry. If, as Ikeda believes, poetry, like life, is a series of pilgrimages, then the pilgrimage each reader of this poet's works is poised to undertake preserves the "dawning sky," the "pure white rose" and the "fairy-tale princess" "even in an era / of disordered humanity" ("To my young friends," p. 25).

Ikeda's approach to life and the poetry he writes betray an Emersonian bias. A lifelong reader of Ralph Waldo Emerson's essays, Ikeda has assimilated into his poetry a rhetorical feature evident in much of Emerson's prose. Just as, in approaching an essay by Emerson, readers know that the point of view being expressed is Emerson's, so too readers approaching a poem by Ikeda know that the point of view being expressed is his. Yet in their respective writings both Emerson and Ikeda empower readers to relate the essay (in Emerson's case) or the poem (in Ikeda's) to themselves, and thus to adapt the writer's expression to their own situation.

Routinely in Emerson's prose, questions asked early on—such as "Where do we find ourselves?" and "How shall I live?"—invite a reader to seek and find a connection between the subject at hand and the course of his or her own life.[2] Similarly, as readers quickly learn, in Ikeda's poetry the pronouns of choice are invariably "I," "you" and "we," so that his poems rhetorically enforce on readers a sense of interconnectedness wherein, as members of the human community, readers and the poet find themselves standing in a great variety of relations to each other, nature and the cosmos, and as they share in Ikeda's expression of his "surprise and emotion" at discovering "such connections," readers may well be inclined to embellish the poet's vision with experiential associations and discoveries of their own.

Emerson and Ikeda's erasure of distance between themselves

and their readers is hardly a gimmick designed to win over readers to their point of view; for both, it is an act of generosity that trusts readers to be truthful with themselves when they read what the author has written, and, especially for Ikeda, it is an act of generosity that entrusts to readers of his poems the license to make a poem as well as the meaning they draw from it their own. In the early 1970s, Ikeda summarily expressed his inclination to write poetry this way:

> Even in this humble structure
> I stand on my own stage
> reciting poetry
> in the palace
> of my heart.
> ("To my young friends," p. 27)

Whether by "this humble structure" Ikeda meant the brevity and simplicity of his poem is of no consequence, nor is his representation of himself as standing on "my own stage"; what is of consequence is that the poetry he writes and recites emanates, as he says, from "the palace / of my heart." Believing that poetry is "the spiritual bond that links humanity, society and the universe," Ikeda trusts completely in the hearts, minds and imaginations of his readers to discern in his verses the lessons that will be of most value to them.[3] Neither a pedant nor, certainly, a skeptic, Ikeda yields to his own mind and heart's "full range of motion" whenever he writes, knowing that, as has been true for him, his readers possess the capacity to engage in a process of "weeding and selection" through which they, along with the poet, can be made "sublimely confident" of their shared "humanity" ("To my young friends," p. 33).

Each in its own way, the three essays that follow explore the "full range of motion" that Ikeda brings to the poems gathered in

Journey of Life. In "'A Wondrous Symphony of Life': Lyricism in the Poems of Daisaku Ikeda," Ronald A. Bosco discusses the origin of lyricism in Ikeda's writings through reference to his familiarity with the lyrical tradition in poetry and prose developed by Ralph Waldo Emerson, Henry David Thoreau and Walt Whitman and then undertakes a reading of several of Ikeda's poems, including a number that he revised extensively over the course of his career, that typically exhibit, but sometimes challenge, the boundaries of that tradition.

In "A New Errand Bearer: Daisaku Ikeda's Poetic Response to Walt Whitman and His Quest for Peace," Kenneth M. Price undertakes a comparative study of the relationship between Whitman's response to the American Civil War and Ikeda's response to Japan's role and fate in World War II. Although Ikeda has produced a substantial body of poetry that has been read in Japan and, in translation, in Europe, throughout Asia and in the United States, Price fills a significant void in readers' responses to Ikeda's poetry by drawing attention to Whitman as the one poet to whom Ikeda may be said to most often "talk back." In his treatment of Japan's vexed role in the occupation of Okinawa during World War II and the United States' occupation of that island nation after the war, Price opens a line of inquiry into Ikeda's writings that had not been previously approached by readers or critics.

Finally, Sarah Ann Wider's "Daisaku Ikeda's Poetry of Encouragement" explores various aspects of Ikeda's poetry that, for her, build on his reliance upon dialogue as the principal means for persons of goodwill to realize and promote a sense of interconnectedness within the human community. Noting that "Ikeda's lifelong commitment to building cultures of peace while actively opposing cultures of violence is fundamentally rooted in a poetic understanding of the world," Wider first explores the fundamental relationship between poetry and action in Ikeda's writings; in subsequent sections of her essay, she draws on the firsthand testimony of Ikeda's professional staff to provide readers with the first extensive examination of the spontaneity and complexity of Ikeda's compositional practices and develops Ikeda's lifelong investment in writing poetry for and on behalf of women and the oppressed.

On behalf of my colleagues and myself, I wish to share with you, our readers of the essays that follow in *Encountering the Poems of Daisaku Ikeda*, the sense of privilege we feel at introducing *Journey of Life: Selected Poems of Daisaku Ikeda* to you. Our essays are not three conclusions we offer for your consideration; rather, we consider them as contributing to the beginning of new thoughts and, possibly, new resolutions in you that ideally will eclipse those we arrive at in our respective essays. Thus, in the spirit of Daisaku Ikeda's confidence in the readers of his poetry, we ask you to consider our essays opportunities for you to enter into your own reading of his poems, make the poems and your readings of them your own, and permit your readings to serve you as occasions to engage in conversation with others about the quality of life you have found expressed and encouraged in that volume of remarkable poetry.

Ronald A. Bosco
Albany, New York
June 2, 2014

Notes

1. Ronald A. Bosco, Joel Myerson and Daisaku Ikeda, *Creating Waldens: An East–West Conversation on the American Renaissance* (Cambridge, Mass.: Dialogue Path Press, 2009), p. 116. Originally published in Japanese: *Utsukushiki seimei—chikyu to ikiru* (Tokyo: Mainichi Shimbun, 2006).
2. Ralph Waldo Emerson, "Experience" and "Fate" in *The Collected Works of Ralph Waldo Emerson*, Alfred R. Ferguson, Joseph Slater, Douglas Emory Wilson, Ronald A. Bosco, et al., eds., 10 vols. (Cambridge, Mass., and London: The Belknap Press of Harvard University Press, 1971–2013), 3:27 and 6:1, respectively.
3. Daisaku Ikeda, "A Plea for the Restoration of the Poetic Mind," *World Tribune*, December 12, 1988, p. 3.

"A Wondrous Symphony of Life": Lyricism in the Poems of Daisaku Ikeda

RONALD A. BOSCO

PREFACE

THE TRIUMPH OF THE HUMAN SPIRIT

Brisk morn in the New World,
the light of dawn
dyes the eastern sky crimson,
brightening endless expanses
of canyon and plain.
The pale mysteries of
obscuring mists
quietly disperse,
revealing the green forest,
its colorful flowers and towering trees—
trees that stretch high into the heavens,
with more than a century of growth,
whose regal bearing speaks of
triumph in struggle after struggle.

Early rising birds dance and sing,
dewdrops on leaves flash gold,
as everything that lives
breathes deep the morning air.

The wind rises to carry off
the fresh energy of growth
—the abundant, vital pulse
arising from these magnificent woods—
transporting it to the clustered skyscrapers,
the very heart of civilization.

Towering timbers of the spirit,
Ralph Waldo Emerson,
Henry David Thoreau,
Walt Whitman—
friends bound by a deep and mutual respect,
Ralph Waldo Emerson,
Henry David Thoreau,
Walt Whitman—
ceaselessly issue the generous
cry of their souls,
a call redolent with the vastness of nature,
into the endless firmament
of humanity.

Proud banner-bearers of the
American Renaissance!
Before their emergence,
the word *I* never had so proud a ring,
the words *to live* were never spoken
with such earnest dignity and grandeur.

Literature is a clear mirror
reflecting the human heart.
It is only when the right person
gives it voice
that the written word can shine
with its true, original brilliance.

The poetry of these men
was never authoritative revelation
conferred from oracular heights.
Rather, their words were like
treasured swords
forged in the furnace of the soul
day by day, blow by blow,
amidst the onslaughts of
suffering and trial.

It is for just this reason that
they have continued to offer
to so many people
—in different lands
and different times—
the strength and courage to live
when they confront the implacable
challenges of life.

"Camerado, this is no book,
Who touches this touches a man . . . "
In these words of Whitman,
fearless poet of the people,
we hear the confidence and pride
that gave birth to
the American Renaissance.

Although they be words on paper,
each phrase and line
earnestly addresses
the innermost being and concern
of every one of us as we face
the unavoidable sufferings
of birth, of aging,
of illness and of death.

"Nothing is at last sacred
but the integrity of your own mind."
Emerson's declaration of
spiritual independence
resounds like a proud,
solemn cry of triumph,
a paean to the
dignity of humankind.

Having left behind
the distractions of the city,
Thoreau began his life in the woods,
on the pristine shores of Walden Pond:
"Only that day dawns to which we are awake.
There is more day to dawn.
The sun is but a morning star."

It is in the vigorous spirit
of taking on new challenges
that youth has always found
its defining pride and place.

As they grappled with
the realities of their times,
Emerson, Thoreau and Whitman
never silenced their leonine roar.
The crisp clarity of their call
aroused long-stagnant minds
urging a complacent society
toward vibrant transformation.

Now a century and some decades later,
their courageous call of conviction
still echoes and resounds—
deep, strong and everlasting.

The workings of nature
are infinite and enduring.
The wisdom that issues
from nature's spring
is likewise limitless.
These great leaders of the
American Renaissance
took untold pleasure
in their dialogues with nature,
drawing from it
the nourishment to live,
the energy to sound
loud alarms for their age.

The word *renaissance* signifies
the radiant triumph of the human spirit,
the full flowering of
the infinite power and potential
of a single individual,

the grand undertaking of constructing
a magnificent sense of self,
a new society.

When the chords of the human heart
resonate with the august tones
of nature's ensemble,
we perform a wondrous symphony of life
whose rhythms vibrate
into eternity.

The same primal laws
permeate the stars that sparkle
in distant constellations
and the inner cosmos
of the individual life;
they are two and yet not two,
indivisibly interwoven . . .

On the azure expanses
of this oceanic renaissance,
the freely intermingling
wind and light
of East and West
generate ever-spreading waves
of harmonious union.

Each form of life
supports all others;
together they weave
the grand web of life.
Thus there really is

no private happiness
for oneself alone,
no sorrow
belonging only to others.

An age in which
all the world's people
enjoy the mutually recognized
dignity of their lives,
savoring days of happiness
in a peaceful society . . .

Such is the world of which
Emerson, Whitman and Thoreau dreamed.
This is the path humanity must pursue in the
twenty-first century.

Let us set out in quest
of the dawn of a new renaissance,
guided on this
vivid journey of inquiry
by two great American scholars.

Together we advance
in the thrilling adventure
to explore the inner human cosmos,
to find new sources of our creativity,
our planet's fresh dawn!

In Whitman's words:
"Allons! we must not stop here."
Let us press on together,

my friends and companions.
And let us sing songs of praise
to life's beauties and wonders
as we go.

July 3, 2006

In boundless gratitude for the literary training
I received from my mentor
(pp. 372–77)

I CHOSE "The triumph of the human spirit" (2006) to preface my essay for a specific reason. Because I most prize him as a lyrical poet, I am warmed to find in this poem composed rather late in his career that Daisaku Ikeda has set in verse a detailed personal account of the origin and purpose of an aesthetic that informs and lends shape to virtually all of his poetry. Ikeda has expressed that aesthetic in prose on numerous occasions, but possibly no more forthrightly than in "A Plea for the Restoration of the Poetic Mind" (1988), an essay he wrote in Japanese that was subsequently printed in an English translation in the *World Tribune*.

The *World Tribune* version appears to report Ikeda using the expressions "the poetic heart" and "the poetic mind" to represent two separate entities. However, "the poetic heart" and "the poetic mind" are actually alternate translations of the term *shigokoro*, the *kokoro* of *shi* (poetry). *Kokoro* is an especially rich term in Japanese, indicating at once the affective, volitional and even rational aspects of the poet's inner life and imagination. To my knowledge, Ikeda has never acknowledged the possibility of a heart-mind disjunction in the poet, and I believe it is crucial to readers' understanding of the essay that follows to appreciate how, in both "A Plea for the Restoration of the Poetic Mind" and his poems, he argues that the poetic heart/mind "is the source of human imagination and creativity." "The gaze of the poet," he writes,

> is directed at the heart, at the mind. He does not see . . . things as mere matter. He converses with the trees and the grasses, talks to the stars, greets the sun, and feels a kinship with all that is around him. In all these things he sees life and he breathes life into them, seeing in the myriad changing phenomena of this world the unchanging principle of the universe. And the poet is free of the fetters imposed by institutions and ideologies: he perceives the unlimited potential of the individual that transcends the trappings of society. He recognizes the bond that links all humankind and intricacies of the invisible web of life. . . . The wellspring of this prolific spirit [is] the "poetic mind."

> The poetic mind is the source of human imagination and creativity. It imparts hope to our life[,] . . . gives us dreams, and infuses us with courage; it makes possible harmony and unity and gives us the power . . . to transform our inner world from utter desolation to richness and creativity.[1]

Ikeda composed "The triumph of the human spirit" to serve as his preface to *Creating Waldens: An East–West Conversation on the American Renaissance*, a volume consisting of eighteen conversations in which he engaged with Joel Myerson and me between 2003 and 2005.[2] Extending from the 1830s through the 1860s and featuring writers such as Ralph Waldo Emerson, Nathaniel Hawthorne, Walt Whitman, Margaret Fuller and Henry David Thoreau, the American Renaissance had captured Ikeda's attention as the period in American literary history that represented perhaps better than any other the flowering of a genuinely national poetic imagination and democratic impulse expressed through belles-lettres composed in concert with the exploration, settlement and cultivation of a "New World" Eden. He expresses this view in the opening of "The triumph of the human spirit":

> Brisk morn in the New World,
> the light of dawn
> dyes the eastern sky crimson,
> brightening endless expanses
> of canyon and plain.
> The pale mysteries of
> obscuring mists
> quietly disperse,
> revealing the green forest,
> its colorful flowers and towering trees—
> trees that stretch high into the heavens,
> with more than a century of growth,
> whose regal bearing speaks of
> triumph in struggle after struggle.
> Early rising birds dance and sing,
> dewdrops on leaves flash gold,
> as everything that lives
> breathes deep the morning air.

As these lines suggest, Ikeda understands and writes geographical America as a lyrical expression. That "The triumph of the human spirit" is his celebration of the aesthetics, philosophy, politics and spirituality of Emerson, Thoreau and Whitman and his embracing of Emerson's and Whitman's poetic theory and practice as precedents for the poetry he writes will not come as a surprise to those familiar with Ikeda's early reading.[3] Although his appreciation of Thoreau would come later, as an adolescent during World War II and as a young man living in the ruins of postwar Japan, Ikeda found in Emerson's Nature (1836) a declaration of the divinity of human life and the universality of thought that traversed the prewar boundaries that separated American from Japanese culture. Having assimilated much from his readings in Platonic thought, in Eastern philosophy and religion and in natural history, in Nature Emerson proclaimed nature the resource through which individuals could restore "original and eternal beauty" to their world and achieve the redemption of their souls.[4] In its appeal to intuition and the senses and in its conviction that language, like any other material fact, is symbolic of a higher spiritual reality that governs the universe, Nature was a crucial first step for Ikeda toward the doctrine of individualism that Emerson eventually defined as "the infinitude of the private man."[5] In nature, as Emerson argued, the individual is always restored to his senses, his thoughts become clear and all limitation associated with his personality is removed when, by entering nature, the individual experiences his finite world transformed into a site of infinite possibility, not only for himself but for all humankind. Emerson's rousing conclusion to Nature articulated that infinite possibility for the generation that included Whitman and Thoreau in a way they never before had heard it expressed:

> Every spirit builds itself a house; and beyond its house, a world; and beyond its world, a heaven. Know then, that the world exists for you. For you is the phenomenon perfect. What we are, that only can we see. All that Adam had, all that Cæsar could, you have and can do. Adam called his house, heaven and earth; Cæsar called his house, Rome; you perhaps call yours, a cobbler's trade; a hundred acres of ploughed land; or a scholar's garret. Yet

line for line and point for point, your dominion is as great as theirs, though without fine names. Build, therefore, your own world.[6]

Informed by his position in *Nature*, Emerson's "The Poet" (1844), an essay that had a profound influence on Whitman's aspiration to be a poet as well as on his theory of poetry, also influenced Ikeda's aesthetics. In "The Poet," Emerson identifies the ideal poet as one who "chaunt[s] [his] own times and social circumstance," serves humankind as its "reconciler" and captures the genius of his nation in verse.[7] We do not have to look beyond Whitman's "Song of Myself" (first published in 1855) to see fulfilled one of Emerson's principal expectations of the ideal poet: that, like Dante, he writes his "autobiography in colossal cipher, or into universality."[8]

In "Song of Myself," Whitman takes up the mission of Emerson's ideal poet, breaking through all barriers of ideology by openly holding "Creeds and schools in abeyance" while, at the same time, embracing "Nature without check with original energy."[9] Because nothing is ever exhausted in Whitman's nature, by approaching nature imaginatively all is possible to both the poet and his reader, including "knowledge of the origin of all poems."[10] In a gesture of radical self-effacement, Whitman, who late in this poem proclaims himself "an acme of things accomplish'd, . . . an encloser of things to be,"[11] yields the personal authority of the poet to the higher authority of his reader's mind and imagination. Immersed in nature, Whitman tells his reader:

> Stop this day and night with me and you shall possess
>   the origin of all poems,
> You shall possess the good of the earth and sun, (there
>   are millions of suns left,)
> You shall no longer take things at second or third
>   hand, nor look through the eyes of the dead, nor
>   feed on the specters in books,

> You shall not look through my eyes either, nor take
> things from me,
> You shall listen to all sides and filter them from
> yourself.[12]

In his extended prose poem *Walden* (1854), Thoreau took Emerson's doctrine of nature in a slightly different direction, writing: "A lake is the landscape's most beautiful and expressive feature. It is earth's eye; looking into which the beholder measures the depth of his own nature."[13] Whereas in their public writings Emerson and Whitman tended to direct their sight outward, in *Walden* Thoreau casts his imaginative gaze inward. Poised on Walden Pond and peering into its depths, Thoreau plumbed the depth of his human nature, and, as he wrote, he was prepared to accept whatever confirmation of self or self-indictment that came his way as he explained the motivation behind his two-year sojourn at Walden Pond:

> I went to the woods because I wished to live deliberately, to front only the essential facts of life, and see if I could not learn what it had to teach, and not, when I came to die, discover that I had not lived. I did not wish to live what was not life . . . nor did I wish to practice resignation. . . . I wanted to live deep and suck out all the marrow of life, to live so sturdily and Spartan-like as to put to rout all that was not life, . . . to drive life into a corner, and reduce it to its lowest terms, and, if it proved to be mean, why then to get the whole and genuine meanness out of it, . . . or if it were sublime, to know it by experience.[14]

As he explored competing "essential facts of life" throughout *Walden*, Thoreau was increasingly surprised—but never disappointed—to discover that, true to what nature discloses, the meanness and the sublimity of life existed in concert with the "savage" and "spiritual" dimensions of his own and others' human nature:

> I found in myself, and still find, an instinct toward a higher, or, as it is named, spiritual life, as do most men, and another toward a primitive rank and savage one, and I reverence them both. I love the wild not less than the good.[15]

Whether as readers we define our particular interest in poetry as the aesthetic, the spiritual or moral, the political or the social well-being of ourselves and our fellows, poets such as Whitman and prose poets such as Emerson and Thoreau speak with all the moral authority of the sacred scriptures of nations. As are the chapters, verses and commandments of those scriptures, the poet's lines are as penetratingly ethical as they are literarily expressive in their comprehensiveness, regardless of the particular subject about which the poet writes.

Because the poet's focus is always on the universal experiences of the human heart, mind and imagination, the poet speaks not just about himself but about all humankind, not just to or about his own time but across the ages. And because from all times and all nations poets speak to us in lines that ultimately blur distinctions between spiritual (or, if you prefer, religious), political, social and even aesthetic theories and our practices of them, poets are as much our inspiring teachers as they are our lawgivers.

As Ikeda's sources on the character of the ideal poet, Emerson, Whitman and Thoreau are men of refined lyrical sensibility who nevertheless do not shy away from challenging their contemporaries to action on the most pressing social issues of their day. Living in the heady and hectic times of mid-nineteenth-century America, when everyday experience confirmed for Americans their ideal conception of their nation as a "great democracy" and established mythic ("Edenic") associations for America that intellectual and literary historians and politicians invoke in modern contexts today, these three intended their poetry as well as their poetic prose to effect an uplifting of the human spirit, even when they themselves read and wrote about their times with brutal candor.

This is a central characteristic of Ikeda's own poetry, which he discovered early in the writings of these three. Additionally, in the self-discovery and self-creation Whitman arrived at through broadcast glances at his contemporaries and their ideals in "Song of Myself," and in Thoreau's self-discovery and self-creation accomplished while peering into the depths of Walden Pond and applying the lessons he gleaned from that metaphorically deeper insight to himself, his contemporaries and the natural landscape around him, Ikeda found in the distant culture of America justification for the moral imperative he applied to the poet and poetry. Because poetry is "the spiritual bond that links humanity, society, and the universe" together,[16] the "poet [who] can perceive the infinite possibilities of humanity" must make his poetry

> a song in praise of humanity. The perception of those possibilities is really the perception of interconnectedness, like that between friends, between humanity and nature, and between humanity and the cosmos. Poetry crystallizes the surprise and emotion of awakening to such connections.[17]

Writing in his journal on May 10, 1853, Thoreau anticipated Ikeda's understanding of the function of poetry and its privileged association with nature by more than one hundred years. "He is the richest," he observed,

> who has most use for nature as raw material of tropes and symbols with which to describe his life. If these gates of golden willows affect me, they correspond to the beauty

and promise of some experience on which I am entering. If I am overflowing with life, am rich in experience for which I lack expression, then nature will be my language full of poetry,—all nature will *fable*, and every natural phenomenon be a myth. The man of science, who is not seeking for expression but for a fact to be expressed merely, studies nature as a dead language. I pray for such inward experience as will make nature significant.[18]

In "The triumph of the human spirit," Ikeda celebrates Emerson, Thoreau and Whitman as "towering timbers of the spirit, / . . . friends bound by a deep and mutual respect," who "ceaselessly issue the generous / cry of their souls, / a call redolent with / the vastness of nature, / into the endless firmament / of humanity." Emerson, Thoreau and Whitman: more than four decades before he composed "The triumph of the human spirit," Ikeda accepted from these "banner-bearers" of the American Renaissance the challenge and the license to, as he wrote, "stand on my own stage / reciting poetry / in the palace / of my heart" ("To my young friends," p. 27), and issue forth a renaissance for his own time, which he often figures poetically through the image of "dawn."

Since the collective gift to humanity of these three writers was that, before their time, "the word *I* never had so proud a ring, / the words *to live* were never spoken / with such earnest dignity and grandeur," Ikeda resolved that the poetry he would write would come from his heart in the confidence that his heart provided him the courage to reject "a life of theorizing / and formality" ("To my young friends," p. 29). Political and social systems born of ideology and literary art born of formalism that momentarily fence in the individual have always occurred across the ages and will continue to occur, yet as Ikeda sees them, their power is at best transitory, for they can never absolutely hedge in the individual intellect or imagination, nor can they ever permanently diminish either the heart or its expression through poetry.

Writing in the second half of the twentieth century and into the first half of the twenty-first, Ikeda is painfully aware of the political and social systems that appear to assault individuals and nations from all sides, but literature—especially lyrical poetry as he practices it—is a mirror "reflecting the human heart" with "true, original brilliance." With theorizing and formality displaced by nature, Ikeda has learned from these champions of the human spirit how to address "the unavoidable sufferings / of birth, of aging, / of illness and of death" with an equanimity that reflects the "infinite and enduring" "workings of nature." As he insists in "A Plea for the Restoration of the Poetic Mind," there is no disjunction between the heart and mind in the poet, for the chief lesson he received from Emerson, Thoreau and Whitman that has guided him throughout his poetic career is,

> When the chords of the human heart
> resonate with the august tones
> of nature's ensemble,
> we perform a wondrous symphony of life
> whose rhythms vibrate
> into eternity.
>
> The same primal laws
> permeate the stars that sparkle
> in distant constellations
> and the inner cosmos
> of the individual life;
> they are two and yet not two,
> indivisibly interwoven . . .

"Blossoms that scatter" (1945) and "August 15—The dawn of a new day" (2001)[19]

Daisaku Ikeda clearly prefers to create lyrical rather than predominantly didactic poems. Yet Ikeda has produced a substantial body of work in both forms, and as I have suggested in my discussion of "The triumph of the human spirit" and "A Plea for the Restoration of the Poetic Mind," he is forthright about speaking directly to his audience in his own voice and, sometimes punctuating it with exclamation marks, making the lesson he wishes to impart evident to readers. For Ikeda, the poet's "gaze" is not so much directed *at* objects but *through* them for the universal truths they have to reveal. Objects are thus invariably symbols or ciphers of the world for this poet, and for him the poet's act of creation always involves his first sight, then his recording of that sight in memory, then his remembrance (and perhaps improvement) of the first sight in periods of contemplation, and then his further internalization through imagination of objects prior to their achieving what I would characterize as the poet's second sight of them in the lines of his verses.

Even in his second-sight report of objects in verse, the poet's sight is always a contingent—always a penultimate—sighting, for once committed to the printed page, the poet's second sight of an object now (re)born of imagination becomes his own and his readers' new object and a new source of first sight. Ikeda often treats the poet's first sight (or later contingent second sighting[s]) of objects as analogous to a photographer's first sight and recording of an object within a frame, and once there—once fixed and framed—it becomes the photographer's and his audience's invitation to a second sight. How often we have said that we have found so much more on our second reading of a book than on our first. Has the book changed? No, we have. And so it is with Ikeda's ideal poets and readers: always a new sight awaits them, for inasmuch as poets and readers are constantly changed by their experiences, they rarely see an object—even one seemingly fixed in a frame—or read their poems the same way they did when they first composed the lines that now contain the object of their sight.

In "Blossoms that scatter" (pp. 3–4) and "August 15—The dawn of a new day" (pp. 340–52), two poems that had a long intellectual and imaginative gestation and were finally composed only after a period of extended reflection and introspection by the poet, Ikeda reprises the soul-inspiring and also highly sobering lessons he learned in his early years and applies them to the increasingly global post-World War II community he initially encounters as a young man and later serves as a champion for peace. "Blossoms that scatter," the earlier of the two pieces, is a powerfully moving lyric in which the poet recreates his original mood and thoughts as he witnessed the spectacle of cherry trees blooming on a spring day in April 1945 amid the ruins of a temple that stood near the site of the bombed-out ironworks where he was a teenage laborer. No doubt, the poet has relived his mood and thoughts of that day many times over and improved the spectacle that he witnessed to be somehow more in concert with a romanticist's view of the order of nature, if only to come to terms with the devastating explosions that wrenched cherry blossoms from their moorings and spread them against the sky in the first place. Throughout this poem, Ikeda's emphasis is on the scattering of the cherry blossoms, and from his opening lines, various manifestations of *scattering* serve as his controlling symbol within the poem:

> Cherries in bloom that the air raid spared
> blue sky above them   fallen petals jumbled
>
> for a background the gutted ruins of reality
> and the pitiful people who cannot look up to them[.]

By contrast, "August 15—The dawn of a new day" is a distinctly non-lyrical poem. Commemorating "*August 15, 1945*— / The day the Japanese nation, / led by arrogant, foolish leaders, / fell in defeat," this poem expands one of Japan's darkest, harshest hours into a lifetime's "day of penitence" that recalls "the senseless / battlefield deaths / of so many millions / of loved ones" as a caution against the foolhardiness of war. Except for Ikeda's confidence that with the passage of time August 15, 1945, may now be read as "the start / of a new era" in which "people's hearts / . . . pulse again with joy / toward a new future," here the poet speaks with a heightened sense of urgency as he returns over and over again to this thought: the line between August 15 as "a day of hopeless heartbreak" and a day of individual and national renewal is a slender, tenuous one. Recognizing that the role of the poet in society is not only to advertise the uplifting, consolatory lessons the lyricist may invoke out of the ruins of the past, but also to assure that his contemporaries never forget that the source of those ruins resides in actions taken out of base human impulses, in "August 15—The dawn of a new day" Ikeda puts into practice the charge he issues to all persons of power in his poem "In Joyous Tumult":

> You who wield power!
> It is up to you
> to offer the world
> the highest example and model.
> By rights you should be poets,
> people of refinement
> and compassion,
> . . . engaged
> in the work of building peace.[20]

Reading both poems through reference to these lines from "In Joyous Tumult," "Blossoms that scatter" appears at thematic odds with "August 15—The dawn of a new day" in one important respect: here, the poet does not use the spectacle before him to counsel his fellows against the inevitable devastation that awaits all in war. "Blossoms that scatter" is thus far less a poem advocating peace than it is a poem offering survivors consolation over the effects of war, and by offering consolation, it remains true to the romantic vision that inspires it. Following his introductory lines, in "Blossoms that scatter" the poet wonders whether the blossoms' explosive scattering through the atmosphere is not itself comparable to the wandering of those parents and children who, displaced by the bombing raid, now find themselves "bitter" as they meander aimlessly "amid the waves of little shacks" where flowers are still in bloom. The mingling of those cherry blossoms that now rain down from the sky as victims of the raid with flowers in bloom that have survived the bombs prompts the poet to ask, "Is theirs the hue of dawn?" "Ah," replies the poet, signaling an insight he has achieved only after an extended period of mature reflection on what he saw that terrible day,

> . . . there is a simile in this existence
> men of power and men of peace
>
> "blossoms that scatter, blossoms that remain
> to become blossoms that scatter"—so sings a man[.]

There is, indeed, a simile in this spectacle discoverable by men of power who are also men of peace, and the simile operates whether one interprets the cherry blossoms as literal cherry blossoms or as emblems of those young men "in distant southern seas," who, as "ill-fated cherries" not yet in "full bloom," endure the agony of their "branches" wracked by painful wounds delivered to them by the instruments of war. Because the cherry blossoms that have scattered and those that remain are part of nature's continuum, those blossoms that remain are akin to those that have scattered to the extent that their brief destiny is to linger on their branches for a while before falling and being "jumbled" and scattered themselves. Nature's answer to the poet's query—"Is theirs the hue of dawn?"—is that the "dawn" both sets of blossoms announce is not entirely a dawn of hope; rather, it is a dawn that accepts as inevitable the fate that awaits the surviving blossoms within nature's continuum. As the poet knows, the surviving blossoms are "blossoms of youth" many million strong, and although he asks "why must they scatter? why must they scatter?" he is reconciled to the inevitability of their fate and urges his "friends remaining" to be reconciled as well to "the loss of the world of the ideal." And in the face of this sobering reality driven home to the poet—and, in turn, by the poet to the reader—at the sight of "the gutted ruins of reality" in which the action of the poem takes place, the poet poses three questions:

> Are all things impermanent? are they eternal?
> without even knowing, must we scatter?

Ultimately, Ikeda answers each of these questions in the affirmative. As a lyrical poem, "Blossoms that scatter" affirms the eternality of all existence by reference to the constancy with which nature both orchestrates change and accepts and survives change regardless of its origin, including change instigated by misguided men who make war. Yes, then, Ikeda the poet says, things are both "impermanent" and "eternal"; and yes, too, he says, we—however "we" is read—must scatter. Thus, while "Blossoms that scatter" may not serve as an argument against war, the poem nevertheless offers an enduring consolatory lesson that the poet has discovered in the "fragrance" of the blossoms that greet every spring "storm," whether the storm arises as an act of nature or from some form of human intervention:

Blossoms that scatter, blossoms that remain,
bloom forever, in spring send out your fragrance on
the storm!

Except that we know that they have come from the same mind and imagination, "Blossoms that scatter" and "August 15—The dawn of a new day" are remarkably different poems, so much so that over repeated readings I sometimes find them oppositional. "August 15" is a poem without a middle ground that the lyrical "Blossoms that scatter" offers in the consolation Ikeda arrives at for himself and his readers. In "August 15," the poet refuses to be reconciled to either war or its effects; in fact, the nearly three decades that separate the first appearance of "Blossoms that scatter" in English in 1976 and the first appearance of "August 15—The dawn of a new day" in English in 2004 suggest that—although I, along with other of his readers, may prefer the lyric capacity of many of Ikeda's poems that have been translated into English—by 2004, the poet may have lost patience with the ease with which lyricism rewrites and thereby seems to lessen the harsh reality of war through naturalistic symbols.

The descriptors Ikeda uses throughout "August 15—The dawn of a new day" extend the dark imagery with which he opens the poem, for his characterization of August 15 as a "day of penitence," "hopeless heartbreak" and "anguished grief" sets the tone for the litany of "bitter tears" and "eternal parting" that follows in the poem. The poet reminds us that in the aftermath of Japan's surrender, politicians wrangled over "Who was responsible? / Who would pay / or make amends / for these crimes" of war that cost the lives of "untold numbers of noncombatants," persons whose "hearts filled / with biting sorrow / and bitter outrage / at the stupidity of war" as they drew their last breaths. Joining the politicians were others who argued about the most fitting memorials to build to honor the service, suffering and courage of "so many men" and "so many women too," who gave their lives to the war. Exasperated by the nonsense of such an argument, however, Ikeda intrudes into his narrative to assert in his own voice:

> More important
> than debating where
> the souls of the fallen
> should be enshrined
> is that we never forget
> the precious reality
> of their lives.

"Everyone is equal / in their humanity," he insists; if this supreme fact—"this principle, this law"—becomes the focus of persons of goodwill and sound judgment in the twenty-first century, then those rationales that were formerly so easily invoked to make the case for war and fret over memorials to it will lose their power before a brand of "fundamental humanism" that has the capacity to change the world.

Although "Blossoms that scatter" evolved out of the poet's personal experience, the heart-wrenching candor of the autobiographical narrative Ikeda develops in "August 15—The dawn of a new day" quite overwhelms the personal aspect of the earlier poem. Recalling the horribly maimed condition of Japan's city- and country-scapes as he witnessed them both during and after the war, the poet laments, "these sights / are burned indelibly / in my heart." This admission ushers in a series of snapshot but unforgettable recollections that Ikeda has carried with him over the years, some drawn from witnessing events that unfolded during successive air raids on already bombed-out streets and others from the forever altered reality of the honest, idyllic family life he had enjoyed as an adolescent before the war. A half-century after the surrender, Ikeda vividly recalls:

"A Wondrous Symphony of Life"

In the midst of an air raid
. . . .
an elderly couple shaking with fear
as they fled weaving their way
through the streets.

Also unforgettable
was this pitiful sight—
a group of middle-aged men,
. . . .
scampering in desperate rout
like trapped and panicked prisoners . . .

. . . .
my four elder brothers,
all in the prime of life,
called away to war.
. . . .
My eldest brother
. . . sent to fight in Burma,
where he died in battle.

. . . .

In those days,
my father and my mother
rarely smiled.
. . . .
It was an era of people
drifting through the streets
lost in solitary sadness.

. . . .

> Everywhere the sight
> of decent people
> looking like those condemned
> to climb the gallows stairs
> at the unfeeling command
> of brutal assassins.

It was a bitter outrage.

In a lengthy pause during the middle of "August 15," Ikeda observes that the "human heart holds / terrible possibilities," so terrible, in fact, that only his nation's utter defeat stays the cloud of darkness that has descended over the lives and fortunes of his countrymen. The day of August 15, 1945, was itself "bright and brilliant"; although some wept at the news of Japan's defeat, "far more," the poet says, "felt relief / deep in their hearts."

As happened to countless families, the Ikedas lost all the earthly possessions that defined their home life, but rather than dwell on their losses, the poet and his family initially found comfort in having "emerged from a / deep and hellish gloom" into a period of "some happiness and cheer." But just as the brilliance of a summer's day is too often transitory, so the cheer that the poet and his family felt at the cessation of hostilities proved fleeting, for the arrival of the news that Kiichi Ikeda—the poet's eldest brother—had died in Burma left the family "tossed down / to misery's depths."

Annually reliving such moments of the war's end for fifty-five years, in "August 15—The dawn of a new day," which he completed and dated on August 14, 2001, Ikeda wrote, "Each year I greet / this day of August 15 / my heart filled with outrage." Although the war "shattered" his family's home life "to misery's depths," the sources of the poet's outrage are not personal—they are universal. "Countless people," he states, "wept tears / of anguished suffering / and heaving grief" throughout the war and after, and speaking of himself, the poet acknowledges that he was hardly alone in having his youthful hopes "ruined, distorted and despoiled" by the avarice and arrogance of elders who sent young men into brutal conflicts that left their "purest sentiments / crushed underfoot." Underscoring the universal destructiveness of the war's long-term aftereffects on his contemporaries, Ikeda shares with us once again the feelings that consume him as August 15 makes its annual return: "With the coming / of this day each year / my sorrow at the pain and loss / turns to boiling rage." That the poet's "heart filled with outrage" has now become the site of "pain and loss" that annually consumes him with "boiling rage" is an empowering admission that allows the poet to pause in his lament and, assuming the voice of the Japanese people, challenge his nation's political, social and religious leaders:

> August 15—
> . . . .
> Is this not the day
> when you should
> vow to consecrate your lives
> to the people
> to the cause of peace,
> the day when you should
> promise to work
> with unstinting devotion
> for the happiness
> of all people?

Although "August 15—The dawn of a new day" lacks the consolatory message of a lyrical poem such as "Blossoms that scatter," it is not a poem without rare intellectual and imaginative power and inspiring resolutions. Having explored to their depths the "terrible possibilities" that the "human heart holds," Ikeda leaves behind but certainly does not forget "the pain and suffering" and "dank prison torture" that "bombardment, / military assault and warfare" collectively imposed on the human condition during World War II and may impose on the human condition again. A consolatory lesson he draws from the war of his youth is "the truth / that demonic evil / plainly contains / the seeds of its own destruction." Based upon personal experience, this lesson piques in him the resolve never to forget August 15, 1945, no matter how difficult the memory of lost family and friends and the loss of pride in national identity represented by that day may be for him:

> August 15—
> We must never forget
> the painful misery of that day.
> We must never forget
> the desolation of that day.
> And we must never forget
> that humiliating awakening
> to the folly of slavish obedience.

In a remarkable, lyrical turn in "August 15—The dawn of a new day," at the opening of a new century, Ikeda transforms all future August fifteenths left to him into "day[s] of fresh departure" and consecrates himself "to work / with unstinting devotion / for the happiness / of all people." The war and its accompanying ravages that stole his youth and tainted too many of what ought to have been opportunities for joy among members of his generation represent the old news of a rapidly receding century. On August 14, 2001, Ikeda dedicated himself entirely to "the youth of the new century," and with a sense of urgency that only the poet's voice can sound, he announced the fact to his readers. Instead of revisiting it ever again as a day of lamentation, Ikeda now improves the negative energy of the past into personal resolutions to mark every future August 15 as the "start of a new era of life" and a memorial "day of peace" "respected by all / the world's citizens." As the historical and autobiographical narrative of "August 15—The dawn of a new day" makes plain, it has taken the greater part of his adult life for the poet to arrive at this position, but finally he has come to the point in his life where his commitment to secure world peace for the spiritual and physical enrichment of all displaces the personal sense of pain, loss and outrage that have colored all of his previous August fifteenths. From the darkness of his own past, the poet thus emerges into the light of a splendid future.

"Fuji and the Poet" (1947) and "Offering prayers at Mount Fuji" (1950/1991)

With their durability and majesty serving as sources of inspiration, mountains have long appealed to the lyrical imagination of artists and poets, an impulse that Daisaku Ikeda shares. The poems and original works of photographic art included in his *Songs from My Heart* (1978) are literally wrapped within an expansive but subtle pastel-hued front cover, spine and back cover photograph of the Himalayas taken from Nepal. In the volume, another of Ikeda's photographs realistically captures an Alpine range of snowy peaks just as white, puffy clouds approach and then gather around their edges. In the volume, too, are two poems that were inspired by Ikeda's sightings of and musings on Mount Fuji: "Mount Fuji and the Poet" (1947) and "Praying to Mount Fuji" (1950), both printed in translations by Burton Watson.[21]

In *Journey of Life: Selected Poems of Daisaku Ikeda*, "Mount Fuji and the Poet" has been superseded by "Fuji and the poet" (pp. 5–6) and "Praying to Mount Fuji" by "Offering prayers at Mount Fuji" (pp. 9–11). Each poem required the Soka Gakkai translation team in Tokyo to prepare new text in English for very different reasons. Lacking a clear sense of Ikeda's debt in the now-titled "Fuji and the poet" to the early twentieth-century Japanese naturalist poet Wakayama Bokusui, translator Burton Watson mistakenly assumed that the text was entirely Ikeda's, and his translation neglected the crucial collaborative gesture Ikeda makes in the poem toward Bokusui, who died in the year that Ikeda was born. By contrast, Watson's "Praying to Mount Fuji" represented a 1970s version in English of a poem that Ikeda afterward returned to and revised in Japanese through 1991. To the extent that any poem is ever truly finished in a poet's mind, "Offering prayers at Mount Fuji" is Ikeda's latest, if not his final, poetic word on the subject.

Written when the poet was nineteen, "Fuji and the poet" is Ikeda's love song to Mount Fuji, and within it he expresses a profound intellectual debt to the elder Bokusui, who was moved to tears by the "mountain's unmatched harmony and splendor." In "Offering prayers at Mount Fuji," the poet's imaginative reach tends outward and his line of sight is enormously broad as he reflects on the mountain's record of history's "pages pile[d] up / thousands, tens of thousands deep" until he discerns in Fuji's symbolically eternal form a consolatory message for the cares and uncertainties of his own life. By contrast, in "Fuji and the poet," Ikeda's gaze is almost wholly inward and developed across his adaptation of and enlargement upon Bokusui's earlier poetic descriptions of Mount Fuji. Thus, while invoking Bokusui as the architect of a vision of Fuji that Ikeda shares and wishes to emulate in his own verse, the poem ultimately becomes a personal expression of how the mountain and Ikeda have complemented and altered each other over repeated interaction.

In "Fuji and the poet," punctuation and the expanse of white space along the right margin create an impression of snapshot images of Mount Fuji that Ikeda—and before him Bokusui—

descriptively committed to memory and Ikeda now reprises in verse. Read aloud, at moments this poem sounds confessional, which it surely is; at other times, it vacillates between the conversationally familiar and the rhapsodic:

Fuji and the Poet

There was a poet, a poet who sang
of this mountain's unmatched harmony and splendor.

> Forgive me, Fuji.
> Tonight as I look up at you
> I find myself weeping, without reason.

There was a poet who focused the light of his seasoned
    skill
on this ultimate of the Earth's forms, and wept.

> A day without wind.
> In the dear and dreamlike emptiness of the sky,
> a cloud is born to long after Fuji.

A poet who loved Fuji through the cycles of great art
that burned in the depths in his life.

Bokusui elevated himself to converse with Fuji
and solemnly sing its infinite melodies.

Fuji under clear skies.
Shining Fuji.
Snow-clad Fuji.
Towering Fuji.

Fuji's crisp outline against the winter sky.
Fuji under rainclouds.
Rough-skinned Fuji.
White-robed Fuji.

Fuji at daybreak.
Cloud-capped Fuji.
Fuji in the bright light of dawn.
Fuji tonight.

Fuji under leaden skies.
Expansive Fuji.
Fuji in the white garb of spring.
Fuji exposed in autumn.

High in the skies he sings his praise
for this mountain of goodness, justice and philosophy.

"Fuji and the poet" is one of Ikeda's foremost and finest demonstrations of his aesthetic theory in practice, and it is an unusually complex work for a poet who was still in the apprentice stage of his craft. Four times in the poem, in his own words, Ikeda directly addresses Bokusui, stating that of the two, Bokusui is the "poet who [first] sang / of this mountain's unmatched harmony and splendor," "who [first] focused the light of his seasoned skill / on this ultimate of the Earth's forms, and wept," "who [first] loved Fuji through the cycles of great art / that burned in the depths in his life," and who first "elevated himself to converse with Fuji / and solemnly sing its infinite melodies."

Twice in the poem, Ikeda directly quotes Bokusui, which has been indicated in the translation by the indentation of lines from the left margin: "Forgive me, Fuji. / Tonight as I look up at you / I find myself weeping, without reason," and "A day without wind. /

In the clear and dreamlike emptiness of the sky, / a cloud is born to long after Fuji."[22]

In the last two lines of the poem, Ikeda appears to acknowledge Bokusui once again as the poet who has imaginatively assimilated and expressed the power of Mount Fuji in a manner to which Ikeda aspires, but he does so without the directness of his previous four invocations of Bokusui's vision and art: "High in the skies he sings his praise / for this mountain of goodness, justice and philosophy." What appears to be missing here is Ikeda's overt deference to Bokusui as the master poet, for the "he" in these lines is as much the poet Ikeda, the author of each of the four quatrain stanzas that precede the last lines of the poem, as it is the poet Bokusui.

Although neither Bokusui nor Ikeda can ever be the sole arbiter of the defining qualities that make Mount Fuji a site of inspiration for poets and others who are moved by its majesty, along with Bokusui, Ikeda has fully assimilated in his own imagination Fuji's variously "Shining," "Towering," "Rough-skinned," "White-robed," "Cloud-capped" and "Expansive" features to compose sixteen lines of original verse that express the intricate web of physical and emotional responses he has to the mountain across both the seasons and his moods. It is in these original verses that Ikeda elevates himself "to converse with Fuji" and inaugurates what will become a lifetime's celebration of Mount Fuji's "infinite melodies."

As also happens in "Offering prayers at Mount Fuji," in "Fuji and the poet" Ikeda engages in an extended pilgrimage of the imagination, but with this difference: in "Offering prayers at Mount Fuji," the mountain and the poet are separated by their respective size and duration in a way that freezes Mount Fuji as an immense and initially unapproachable object upon which the poet gazes, while in "Fuji and the poet," the distance between the two is initially reduced by Ikeda's assimilation of Bokusui's poetic sharing of his privileged insights on and relation to Fuji, and that distance is reduced even further by Ikeda, who has assimilated

Fuji and its power within himself in response to Fuji's extending to him its natural wonder and representative "goodness, justice and philosophy."

Reading "Fuji and the poet" through reference to poetic models Ikeda identifies in "The triumph of the human spirit," one finds that this poem offers evidence of an epiphany on Ikeda's part comparable to that Emerson described in *Nature*, where, transformed into a "transparent eye-ball" in which all egotism vanishes, the narrator asserts that the currents of universal being flow within him.[23] But "Fuji and the poet" is not Emersonian in the final analysis; instead, the poem appears to correspond perfectly to Thoreau's dictum, "I pray for such inward experience as will make nature significant,"[24] and to the extent that it does, "Fuji and the poet" reveals that the prayers Ikeda offers to Mount Fuji in his later poem would appear to have been answered in this earlier one. For here, the poet initially approaches Fuji through Bokusui's eyes and verses as well as through his own experience of the mountain and in expressions he has assimilated from Bokusui's writings, yet, although he is an apprentice, Ikeda already knows that neither Bokusui nor he can ever exhaust the imaginative possibilities Mount Fuji offers an individual open and receptive to its power. Making that concession, the poet and Mount Fuji ultimately collaborate through the multiple sources of Ikeda's personal experience of the mountain to make this poem.

An essential lesson that Ikeda expresses in "Fuji and the poet" is that the mountain has already transferred to the poet its "key to reveal the secrets of the cosmos" ("Offering prayers at Mount Fuji"). Optimistically exulting in a mood reinforced by his observation of the constancy of Mount Fuji's love toward poets across all ages, in this early poem Ikeda imaginatively embraces the mountain for the "unmatched harmony and splendor" in which it stands before him in an act of love, and, extending the legacy he inherits from Bokusui, he, too, weeps with joy at Fuji's offering to his consideration the "ultimate of the Earth's forms" and pledges to "solemnly sing its infinite melodies."

As a "mountain of goodness, justice and philosophy," the problems of existence as he perceived them in "Blossoms that scatter" or for over a half-century inwardly suppressed until he could write them out for all to share in "August 15—The dawn of a new day" are simplified to the point that now the poet can meet on his own the ethical challenges of life to which he turns to Mount Fuji for guidance. Indeed, in his erasure of distance between Mount Fuji and himself in "Fuji and the poet," Ikeda fulfills the desired end Thoreau recorded in his journal for the ideal outcome of "inward experience": "I wish to be made better."[25]

In "Offering prayers at Mount Fuji," Ikeda's interest in Fuji's capacity to awaken new levels of spiritual awareness in the observer is signaled by his introductory overtures to the mountain's "light of the day everlasting," "melodies of sacred teachings" and "rhythmic vitality of life," all of which he figures here as "The dawn! The dawn!" With its specific meaning left ambiguous early in the poem, Mount Fuji's "power" is described as both latent and active: it is latent in the sheer magnitude and magnificence of the spectacle the mountain impresses on the thoughtful observer, and active in the creative possibilities for new life, new thoughts and new ethical resolutions in the observer represented by the new dawns that Fuji's physical and symbolic permanence confirms are yet to come.

Comparable to Emerson's conviction that "Every spirit builds itself a house; and beyond its house, a world; and beyond its world, a heaven,"[26] here Ikeda expresses his confidence that, by virtue of its durability, Mount Fuji serves as humankind's symbol of heaven as across its changing seasons the mountain refreshes all nature and is itself refreshed with new birth; the countless dawns Mount Fuji has witnessed and the countless dawns the mountain will witness in ages yet to come hint of the spiritual, if not also physical, perfection toward which humankind is patiently evolving. Ikeda writes,

> . . . rhythmic vitality of life
> brimming with vast and magnificent strength.
>
> Mount Fuji, like the dawn,
> brings restoring richness to our lives.
> It enfolds a soul, eternally enduring.
> Its solemn form like a wise philosopher
> arising from deepest meditation.
> Its peaceful aspect remains unmoved
> by the bravest north winds.
> With the accumulation of propitious snows
> it paints a picture of sacred purity.
> Under the fierce heat of summer's red emperor
> it never neglects to refresh us
> with fragrant breezes and tranquil green.
> Mount Fuji! How transcendent is your perfectly
>   formed beauty!

Praying and meditating at this holiest of sites where pilgrims, prophets and poets have paused in passing across the ages and where new generations of the same still visit in awe, Ikeda embarks on a pilgrimage of the imagination in which he discerns and then accepts the immutable in the mutable, permanency in change. In the rocky lines of Mount Fuji's grand peaks and scarred valleys, he reads history's "pages" "thousands, tens of thousands deep." To his chagrin, the poet reads in those pages symbols of the violence of war and war's doleful effects as the "trampling march of fire and steel," the passage of time as the "sad and tragic currents" on which humanity remains "adrift" while people "yearn" for "firm and certain direction" in their lives, and "the burning house of our all-consuming age" as merely extending the worthlessness of those material "rich robes of the past [that] are now threadbare."

Ikeda feels the pain and relief of the people of the Middle Ages who, "abiding on the parched earth," found spiritual and intellectual sustenance in "the clear waters of Scholasticism" and of "the Jewish people" who, "struggling . . . through harsh trials," "kept faith in the coming of the Messiah / and were filled with the vital breath of life." Then, in the midst of his brief litany of human woe that has been no more than partially relieved across the ages, the poet also remembers "the people of Asia" who, "exhausted by wandering on confounded paths," "encountered the sage philosopher of Eagle Peak." That encounter, of course, refers to the people's "new flowering" under the influence of the Lotus Sutra preached by Shakyamuni in ancient India; the poet's remembrance of it instills in him even greater awe than he has already expressed for "the sacred peak of Mount Fuji" and a heartfelt desire to "bring succor to the suffering" whose spirits are still being battered in the "waves of [our] defiled age / [that] rage ever more ferociously."

Along with his pledge before Mount Fuji to devote himself to bringing "succor to the suffering," Ikeda imaginatively hears in the mountain's "stirring chime" "the tones of freedom, peace and dignity" and resolves to awaken in himself and others "the realities of the inner life" set forth in the Lotus Sutra. In an unexpected turn, he apostrophizes Mount Fuji and accepts the mountain's heritage as providing him with a "key" that "reveal[s] the secrets of the cosmos":

> How incomparable, Mount Fuji!
> Preserving the writings of the great sage,
> home to the eternal guide and master!
> . . . .

Heritage unbroken over so many seasons,
key to reveal the secrets of the cosmos!

Then, returning to the figure of "The dawn! The dawn!" with which he opened "Offering prayers at Mount Fuji," the poet exclaims, "The dawn is here! . . . / The time of humanity's awakening / is finally at hand!" To the extent that Ikeda's purpose in "Offering prayers at Mount Fuji" may be seen as comparable to Thoreau's search for "inward experience" through which "to be made better," the poet's prayers offered at Mount Fuji have been answered. Although Ikeda states, "I have no taste for the exaggerated claims / of narrow particularism," this poem, which—because it is an extended revision of an earlier piece—represents the poet's second- or later-sight encounter with Mount Fuji, serves him and his readers as the site in which he articulates a poet's embrace and fulfillment of Fuji's "stirring chime" as both his personal mission in life and the mission he would share with all like-minded persons of goodwill.

"Pampas grass" (1971) and "Pampas grass, the poet's friend" (2007)

As Daisaku Ikeda admirably demonstrates in "Fuji and the poet" and "Offering prayers at Mount Fuji," a poet's imaginative assimilation of natural objects as means to arrive at universal truth and a sense of the permanent has the potential to satisfy his and his audience's search for ethical resolutions. Both poems reveal Ikeda engaged in acts of spiritual renewal, and as models of the humanistic ideal to which he subscribes, he generously offers them as gifts to humanity. To portray their belief in permanence by symbolizing it through the mutable in their poetry, nineteenth-century lyrical poets adhering to the romantic tradition invoke either the regenerative constancy of nature by reference to the cycle of the seasons or the durability of nature in figures such as the seas' perpetual rise and fall or the seeming eternality of objects such as the first growth forests of North America or Mont Blanc in the French Alps.[27]

Just as seas ebb and flow and mountains are altered by storms as well as by periodic seismic activity, individuals and their cultures are always changing, always growing—hopefully, always for the better. Our experiences and the new knowledge they bring us are transformative moments. As we develop over the course of our lives, the cultures to which we belong and contribute develop in concert with us. For the romantic imagination, the permanency of change is an emblem of infinity and immortality.

Although neither infinity nor immortality can be grasped in this world except by reference to naturalistic symbols or spiritual faith, the lyric poet knows better than others that naturalistic symbols and spiritual faith have the capacity to reawaken in human beings innocence and trust, to instruct them in the virtues of goodness and justice and the value of respect for the ideas and opinions of others, and to inspire in them resolutions to be "made better." Occupying a charmed universe as Ikeda does in "The triumph of the human spirit," the lyric poet imaginatively penetrates nature's broad landscape and discovers it filled with figures that personify his own physical and spiritual experiences and express his own ambitions, desires and fears.

Ikeda eloquently captures this process in "Pampas grass" (pp. 40–42). Described as "listening in stillness" while high and low notes rise through the air over a hilly landscape as someone plays a *biwa* in the distance, pampas grasses arranged in clumps rise "tall and straight" to take notice of the flowing lute-like tune as well as of the flow of the poet's imaginative musings. Early on, the poet wonders whether two stands of the grass within a larger gathering are "a prince who gave his life for the realm" and "a princess who languished for love," who "have emerged from the world of shadows / to take [the] form" of pampas grasses. Nestled among grasses that the poet observes, the prince and princess are not lonely, for they have brought along with them many pampas "retainers / arrayed in spike-plumed finery." Soon, however, the prince and princess merge indistinctly with the other grasses, and once there, they, along with their former "retainers," become collective emblems of the human race. They are nature's beings, and although the poet questions whether they may be weary of their existence, the grasses seem anything but weary as they wander from home to home in "their flowing green trousers" and finally, in this poem, "come to rest and set down roots / among the mountains." Here, with their graceful plumed tops, "wire-thin legs," "arms of silver" and "faces of gold," the innocent pampas grasses literally call the poet—and through the poet, the reader—to join them.

How, exactly, does the pampas grass call? Does this emissary of nature have particular lessons to deliver to us? If so, what has the pampas grass to say about the human condition, which, for the moment, it represents?

The call of the pampas grass first attended to by the poet in "Pampas grass" is integral to the act of imagination that creates this poem. Once the poet has fully assimilated the scene before him, a scene that later in the poem he likens to "delicately stroked patterns / of gold-tipped brush on lacquer" without which details of the pampas grasses' "lives / would have been lost," he recreates for us the musings he has been inspired to undertake by the call to which this scene in nature has alerted him. Instead of a painter's brush preserving his encounter with the splendid grass for future viewings, the poet captures the pampas grass in words through which he reprises the magical exuberance of his own sighting of it and such lessons drawn from that sighting which he has entrusted to his memory, reflected upon and now shares with us.

The lessons of the pampas grass are those associated with the ebb and flow of all life, which, like "the wind[,] blows over the path

/ of flourishing and decline." Wondering whether the pampas grass yearns "to clasp the sleeve / of one now gone," the poet invites us to consider our own longings and losses.

The subject associated with longing and loss that the poet seizes upon is childhood, a subject of universal interest for romantics. Speaking for himself, the poet reflects on memories of his childhood, both those he holds dear, such as the sighting of a harvest moon as impressive as any ever captured on canvas by an artist, and those former "dreams of moon-viewing," once the happy companions of his childhood sleep that now, in his maturity, too often bring him "only sadness" at their loss. Fancying that the autumn wind sweeps "the path of glory and decay," we, as has the poet before us, may read in the wanderings of the pampas grass beyond bamboo thickets, along roadsides, across open plains and in the mountains where they now have settled signs of our personal wandering and mortality and begin to consider the course we will take for the remainder of our life. Yet in the refreshing notice the poet provides to the effect that, even "in the face of frigid gusts" at summer's end, the pampas grasses "shed tears of jeweled dew / opening their plumes," we, like the pampas, may be consoled of our losses and redeemed of our longings through our interaction with nature and engagement in acts of imagination.

The poem ends with the two questions with which the poet has wrestled since first sighting the pampas grass. Although a didactic writer would answer those questions for the reader, Ikeda leaves it to readers to answer those questions for themselves. How an individual answers the questions that follow establishes the quality of the life that will mark that individual's remaining days:

> Do you choose to live in high-minded dignity
> by roadsides and embankments,
> shunning the paths trod by youth?

Or do you live taking in the sight
of those who, in the springtime of life,
flower and rise to new heights?

Most readers would agree that Ikeda's own answer to these questions is to "live taking in the sight / of those who, in the springtime of life, / flower and rise to new heights"; indeed, reading this poem in the company of others of his lyrical poems, it would seem impossible for Ikeda to sustain an argument that favored his—or anyone else's—decision to stand in arrogant aloofness "by roadsides and embankments, / shunning the paths trod by youth." In this respect, "Pampas grass" shares a hopeful tone and thematic kinship with another significant lyrical poem: William Wordsworth's "Ode: Intimations of Immortality from Recollections of Early Childhood" (1802–04).[28] Opening the poem, Wordsworth recalls that,

> There was a time when meadow, grove, and stream,
> The earth, and every common sight,
>   To me did seem
>   Apparelled in celestial light,
> The glory and the freshness of a dream. (ll. 1–5)

But, Wordsworth observes, with the accumulation of experience and the passage of time, the "things which I have seen I now can see no more" (l. 9). Although he tries to hold fast to the idealism of youth, which this poet calls "Nature's priest" (l. 72), at length the adult man perceives that his idealism must inevitably "die away / And fade into the light of common day" (ll. 75–76). This, according to Wordsworth, is ever the course of mortal life, yet the consolation the adult takes from his experience of it is that,

> . . . though the radiance which was once so bright
> Be now for ever taken from my sight,

> Though nothing can bring back the hour
> Of splendour in the grass, of glory in the flower;
>   We will grieve not, rather find
>   Strength in what remains behind;
>   In the primal sympathy
>   Which having been must ever be;
>   In the soothing thoughts that spring
>   Out of human suffering;
>   In the faith that looks through death,
> In years that bring the philosophic mind. (ll. 177–86)

Wordsworth's "philosophic mind" is the mind of acceptance, the mind that comprehends that, regardless of the passage of time, something remarkable and durable ever remains in the human spirit. Against the receding dreams of youth stands—as does Ikeda's "tall and straight" pampas grass—a "primal sympathy": a conviction that what has been "must ever be." Countering the processes of time and degeneration are, for Wordsworth, hopeful "soothing thoughts" of eternity and regeneration. For both Wordsworth and Ikeda, by enduring all change, the human heart in concert with nature serves humankind as priest and mentor, supplying the race with "soothing thoughts" of fresh days and new generations yet to come. In the human heart, Wordsworth finds "the faith that looks through death"—the faith that believes "the meanest flower that blows can give / Thoughts that do often lie too deep for tears" (ll. 202–03); so, too, in the human heart attuned to the notes of the *biwa* heard by the simple, anthropomorphized pampas grass, Ikeda locates the supreme consolation of life.

Just as through the exercise of his imagination the poet receives the long-tested and perennially reborn wisdom of the pampas grass, his poem transmits that wisdom to us. Out of the seeming forlornness and decline depicted in "Pampas grass," the poet affirms life as he bears witness first to the endurance of the pampas grass across time and then to a new generation of persons who will never lose sight of that springtime in which they first flowered and rose to new heights.

The process Ikeda represents in "Pampas grass" is his personal version of the enduring lessons and vivifying consolations lyrical poetry offers humankind. On the eve of his eighties, nearly forty years after composing "Pampas grass," he returned to the figure of the pampas grass in a new poem, "Pampas grass, the poet's friend" (pp. 378–83). Hardly a poem written to concede the woes associated with old age, "Pampas grass, the poet's friend" is a panegyric that affirms life.

In this autobiographical poem, Ikeda is the perennial optimist who writes convinced that his own answer to the questions he posed to readers at the conclusion of "Pampas grass" has borne him in good stead: he has chosen to remain centered in the promise of "the springtime of life" to which the grass beckons, and as experience has taught to him, while there is life, there are always opportunities for individuals to "flower and rise to new heights" as long as they are willing to embrace and act on them. This is the faith and the consolation of the lyric poet; never a doubter or a complainer, never losing his awareness of the transitoriness of life that culminates in death, the lyric poet consciously directs his gaze through the ephemeral back onto life. In "Pampas grass, the poet's friend," Ikeda writes himself brimming with life in concert with nature, whose regenerative capacity symbolizes the faith he embraces to answer the apparent chaos and depression too often associated with everyday human affairs by affirming life and confidence in the infinite possibilities for new life in the future. This, as he expresses at the outset of the poem, is the spirit in which the poet has returned in the autumn of his life to celebrate the pampas grass one more time:

> The pampas grass
> lifts its hands
> in invitation.
> In the sacred solemnity
> of the morning light,
> in the burnished
> sparkle of sunset,
> the pampas grass beckons:
> "Happiness awaits you here!"

Acknowledging that "No one raises / loud cheers for / the pampas grass," Ikeda explains that the fault should not be laid to the pampas grass but to those who fail to appreciate the "noble spirit / with which it strives, / with its slender stalk of life, / to offer [all] the gift / of heartfelt courage / and happiness." Still nature's emissaries, pampas grasses "embody the spirit / of poetry / and friendship" and express through their durability a "nearly human wisdom" as they "offer comfort / to the greatest hearts."

In the morning of our life, their tenacious hold on life "call[s] out brightly" to us, "This way, everyone, this way," with the assurance that there are as many "ways" available to us as there are days to our lives; in the evening of our life, "rustling in the breeze / they commend the triumph / of our day's work and / . . . assure us in whispers / that they will watch over us / in our sleep." Alone, a single pampas grass "feels forsaken," for the strength of pampas grass is its life within a community of fellow pampas grasses. There, they "thrive" in "large and vibrant families, / mutually assisting" one another and "flowering with rich confidence." In the company of "great numbers" of their "children, relations and friends," pampas grasses smile and converse together, exhibit "in the core of their being" that "they are stronger than / the mightiest tree," and model for humankind in their "good-natured," "deeply caring" sense of justice an "inner nobility" worthy of our emulation. And, according to Ikeda, what makes the pampas grass the poet's friend is that, just as the "full moon," "innumerable stars" and "the sun" cast their gaze "on the swaying pampas grass," so, too, humankind may call to mind the humility and strength of this emissary of nature "unconquered by any gale" whenever they become overly complacent in times of joy or needlessly dispirited in times of suffering.

Conclusion: Life in Poetry

The last poem gathered in *Journey of Life: Selected Poems of Daisaku Ikeda* is "Salute to poets" (2007) (pp. 389–95). It is wholly appropriate that in closing this volume Daisaku Ikeda has chosen to acknowledge the authority of poets whose "power in words" possesses an "infinite" capacity "to revive, restore / and make life blaze anew." Although Ikeda would never say this about either his role as a poet in society or his intention for the lyrical poetry he writes, there is no question in my mind that his emphasis throughout the numerous lyrical poems he has written has been to "make life blaze anew," both intellectually and imaginatively, as much for himself as for those who would turn to his poems in their search for enduring lessons through which to measure the quality of their lives and thought and to make a positive difference in the quality of the life and thought of all with whom they interact in this world. In this respect, the theme of "Salute to poets" strikes me as less about poets in general than about the poet who resides in the respective hearts and imaginations of each and every one of us; put another way, given its claim that,

> There is a life in poetry,
> a limitless, eternal life
> that can stir and arouse
> a society to new vibrancy[,]

the subject matter of this poem constitutes an appeal to the heart, mind and feeling of every reader who encounters it.

The fact that the poems by Ikeda which I have emphasized through this essay are lyrical expressions that originate in the feeling and imagination that reside in the poet's heart/mind does not mean that they are fantasies. As I often remind my students, especially those who are not too fond of lyrical poetry, lyricism is an expression in verse of how a poet approaches, processes, assimilates and reflects on the reality of the world he encounters. Against a world described in "Salute to poets" in which a poet witnesses "people / fleeing in confusion / through a field of battle," "a wailing mother / tenderly cradling / a tiny corpse," "the trembling fist / of a young boy, / who writhes beneath / the crushing weights of / discrimination and hate," "the self-mocking sighs / of young people / filled with mistrust and isolation, / who sense no future / as they wander aimlessly," and "the painful cry of Earth herself, / oceans and atmosphere polluted, / stripped and denuded of green, / bound by atomic burdens, / crying in distress," the lyricist announces, "there is / no misery or cruelty / beyond our power / . . . to resolve." The lyric poet can make such a boast, for in his heart of hearts he lives in the confidence that

> All people
> hold within themselves,
> . . . .
> a golden sun
> that can brightly light their own lives
> and shed far and wide
> warm and brilliant beams
> of friendship and fraternity.
> This inner luster
> of life itself,
> is the ultimate

font and source
of new creation.

Believing that "words are / the human heart," in a moment of lyrical exuberance Ikeda challenges poets to "use the words / of compassion and truth" and "universal justice" "to dispel / the dark and heavy clouds / of language laden with / false and evil intent" in order "to stir new winds / of hope and courage" that will usher in a "new and golden dawn!" Yet here the challenge Ikeda issues is directed not only to poets but also to their readers. Readers, too, are human beings who possess a "poetic spirit" that "beats and throbs / in [their] veins"; like Whitman's empowered readers who "shall listen to all sides and filter them from yourself,"[29] Ikeda's readers are empowered by their capacity for "mutual love" and "coming together / in harmonious unity" to "live out their lives / in happiness and dignity," even as they collaborate with and extend on their own the intention of poets to bring "happiness and dignity" to the lives of all they touch.

"A salute to poets" is thus Ikeda's expression of faith in poets *and* their readers who act on the poetic heart/mind. His is a faith that originates in knowledge born of experience that, although "Life is a succession / of painful realities," speaking in his own voice on behalf of poets and their readers, Ikeda asserts, in poetry "I have built a golden life of the spirit / beyond the power of / anyone to destroy" ("To my young friends," p. 28).

NOTES
1. Daisaku Ikeda, "A Plea for the Restoration of the Poetic Mind," *World Tribune*, December 12, 1988, p. 3.
2. Ronald A. Bosco, Joel Myerson and Daisaku Ikeda, *Creating Waldens: An East–West Conversation on the American Renaissance* (Cambridge, Mass.: Dialogue Path Press, 2009). Originally published in Japanese: *Utsukushiki seimei—chikyu to ikiru* (Tokyo: Mainichi Shimbun, 2006).

3. See Daisaku Ikeda, *Wakaki hi no dokusho* (The Readings of My Youthful Days) (Tokyo: Daisan Bunmeisha, 1978) and Daisaku Ikeda, *Zoku, wakaki hi no dokusho* (The Readings of My Youthful Days, continued) (Tokyo: Daisan Bunmeisha, 1993) for his early familiarity with Emerson's essays and Whitman's poetry.
4. Ralph Waldo Emerson, *The Collected Works of Ralph Waldo Emerson*, Alfred R. Ferguson, Joseph Slater, Douglas Emory Wilson, Ronald A. Bosco, et al., eds., 10 vols. (Cambridge, Mass., and London: The Belknap Press of Harvard University Press, 1971–2013), 1:43.
5. Ralph Waldo Emerson, *The Journals and Miscellaneous Notebooks of Ralph Waldo Emerson*, William H. Gilman, Ralph H. Orth, et al., eds., 16 vols. (Cambridge, Mass., and London: The Belknap Press of Harvard University Press, 1960–82), 7:342.
6. Emerson, *The Collected Works of Ralph Waldo Emerson*, 1:44–45.
7. Ibid., 4:21.
8. Ibid.
9. Walt Whitman, "Song of Myself" in *A Textual Variorum of the Printed Poems*, Sulley Bradley, Harold W. Blodgett, et al., eds., 3 vols. (New York: New York University Press, 1980), 1:1, sect. 1, ll. 10, 13.
10. Ibid., 1:2, sect. 2, l. 33.
11. Ibid., 1:71, sect. 44, l. 1148.
12. Ibid., 1:2–3, sect. 2, ll. 33–37.
13. Henry D. Thoreau, *Walden* in *The Writings of Henry D. Thoreau*, J. Lyndon Shanley, ed. (Princeton, N. J.: Princeton University Press, 1971), p. 186.
14. Ibid., pp. 90–91.
15. Ibid., p. 210.
16. Ikeda, "A Plea for the Restoration of the Poetic Mind," p. 3.
17. Ikeda in *Creating Waldens*, p. 116.
18. Henry D. Thoreau, *The Journal of Henry D. Thoreau*, Bradford Torrey and Francis H. Allen, eds., 14 vols. (Boston: Houghton, Mifflin & Co., 1906), 5:135.
19. In the discussions that follow, poems are dated according to the year they were initially composed or, after a period, revised by Ikeda. For details on the dates of initial composition, subsequent revision and publication of poems discussed in this essay, see the Translator's Note and notes to individual poems in *Journey of Life: Selected Poems of Daisaku Ikeda*. Here, I should like to express my sincere gratitude to

Professor Jay Heffron, Ms. Clarissa Douglass and students Yuan Hung Wu, Ranya Maaliki and Hidemi Nishio for facilitating my several discussions on Ikeda's poetic theory and practice at Soka University of America in November 2013 among themselves and the following students: Wai-ki Fong, Nikki Inamine, Satoshi Inuzuka, Yoko Kumano, Masae Kuroki, Minami Muraoka, Yoshiko Ogushi, Zuleyka Shahin and Sachiyo Takahashi.

20. Daisaku Ikeda, "In Joyous Tumult" in *Fighting for Peace*, Andrew Gebert, trans. (Sonoma, Calif.: Dunhill Publishing, 2004), p. 51; "In Joyous Tumult" serves as a companion piece to "August 15—The Dawn of a New Day" in *Fighting for Peace*.

21. Daisaku Ikeda, *Songs from My Heart*, Burton Watson, trans. (New York and Tokyo: Weatherhill, 1978), pp. 54, 37–38, respectively. This volume was first published in its original Japanese version and English translation in deluxe editions by Seikyo Press, Tokyo, 1976.

22. "Forgive me, Fuji" and "A day without wind," trans. from Wakayama, Umi no koe (Voice of the Sea) in *Wakayama Bokusui zenshu*, vol. 1 (Shizuoka, Japan: Zoshinkai, 1992), p. 34.

23. Emerson, *The Collected Works of Ralph Waldo Emerson*, 1:3.

24. Thoreau, *The Journal of Henry D. Thoreau*, 5:135.

25. Ibid., 9:208.

26. Emerson, *The Collected Works of Ralph Waldo Emerson*, 1:44–45.

27. See, for example, "A Forest Hymn" (1825) by the American poet William Cullen Bryant and "Mont Blanc: Lines Written in the Vale of Chamouni" (1816) by the British poet Percy Bysshe Shelley.

28. William Wordsworth, "Ode: Intimations of Immortality from Recollections of Early Childhood" in *English Romantic Writers*, second edition, David Perkins, ed. (New York, London, Tokyo: Harcourt Brace, 1995), pp. 331–34; all quotations from this poem cited by line number(s) in the text are drawn from this edition.

29. Whitman, *Leaves of Grass*, 1:2–3, sect. 2, ll. 33–37.

A New Errand Bearer: Daisaku Ikeda's Poetic Response to Walt Whitman and His Quest for Peace

KENNETH M. PRICE

PREFACE

LIKE THE SUN RISING

Offered to Walt Whitman, poet of the people, on the centenary of his passing, with affection and respect

Like the sun rising
shattering the dark
of old restraints—
with new words, new forms
the soul's liberator
lauds a new world, a new humanity;
sings out democracy's dawn.

Walt Whitman, poet of the people—
you raise your voice

in sonorous praise
of the common people, unknown and unnamed.

America in "the middle range
of the nineteenth century"—
echoing with hammers
pealing the song of construction.
Into the chaos and hope
emerges a man
in his hand a small quarto of poems—
the scant ninety-five pages
of *Leaves of Grass*.

Marking departure from
the civilizations of the Old World,
heart athrob at the thought
of a birthing New World,
prophet of a new age
prolocutor of new ideals.

In your own confident words you are
"Walt Whitman, an American, one of the roughs,
   a kosmos,
Disorderly fleshy and sensual . . . eating drinking
   and breeding . . ."—
intensely human embodiment
of America's freedom,
you are buoyant and rustic,
filled with compassion.

Thick-chested with tempered steel-like arms,
sunburnt face framed

by wildly tousled white hair
and the untrammeled flow of your beard;
beneath thick rich eyebrows
in your clear bright eyes
burns a piercing untamed light—
intelligent and caring.

Your breast's crucible
overflows with the
bright red passion to build
a democratic future.
Your penetrating gaze takes in
the vast universe within
and the signs and promise
of a shining tomorrow.

Everything in the universe
is the subject matter for your poetry—
sky, ocean, mountain, river . . .
even a single grain of sand, even a solitary leaf
the stillness of the wild, the noisy bustling city . . .

You seek out your muse
in ships, in railroads, in tall buildings
in all things everywhere.

You applaud and praise all people—
the young, the old, men and women.
Those whose sweat builds the future,
the widowed wife,
the defeated revolutionary,
the prisoner in jail . . .

You sing the song of,
you sing in praise of
every person on our planet,
the unadorned,
the natural human being.

"Camerado, this is no book,
Who touches this touches a man."
Just so! Your poems flow from
your own overbrimming soul—
they are your very life!

But ah, the critical gales
that beset pathfinders, those who go first!

Because of their revolutionary newness
Leaves of Grass
the songs of your soul
are showered with ridicule and abuse—
"Nauseating drivel."
"As unacquainted with art as a hog
is with mathematics."
"Monster!"

The only words of support and praise
come from the philosopher Emerson
and a handful of people
of discernment and courage.

To you, however, soaring mountainous
the critics' clamorous attacks
are only the murmur of the wind
passing at your feet.

Unheeding of the animadversions
of literati clinging to vain authority
the poet spends his days
quiet and composed
conversing with nature on Long Island.

You do not sing to please the critics;
you sing for the common people
sinking their roots like weeds
into the rich American earth,
secret possessors
of vibrant powers
of birth and renewal;
the people, despised and trampled
driven from history's visible stage.

No one is another's master
no one another's slave—
politics, learning, religion, art
all exist for the human being
for the sake of the people.
To undo the prejudice of race
to break down the walls of class
to share freedom and equality with the people—
it is for this that you sing
to the last limits of your strength.

Your songs—
the Declaration of Humanity
for a new age.

You are the greatest lover
of the common people,

are yourself one
of the proud uncrowned mass
throughout your life.

Your elder brother ill in spirit,
at age eleven you went out
into the world, worked—
as a waiter, a printer, a teacher, reporter . . .
These arduous years
amidst the bitter realities of society
pushed out your bark and
swelled your timber-girth.
From those days of trial and enduring
you learned life's preciousness,
gained nutriment to grow
into a lofty tree of humanism.
Truly only he who has shivered in the cold
can know the sun's warmth.

Ah, your noble altruism!
In the agonized vortex
of the Civil War
you rushed from place to place
nursing the wounded
equally, without distinction between
the soldiers of the North
and those of the South.

Regal in your humanity,
august and proud
like the sky-traversing sun—
smiling, you walk the orbit
of your conviction.

Your verse is like
a clear and optimistic sky
without a single sentimental cloud,
like cresting billows dancing
across an ocean plain—
expansive, energetic, free . . .
Unfettered by the past
you move forward, always forward
toward a future
resounding with hope.

True cheer, true brightness
is the flash of an illumined spirit
resolved in its convictions
piercing the dark night of grief.

Behold Whitman after the war!
Forced to witness
corruption and decay
gnawing at the heart
of the young democracy;
listen to his maddened wail and lament
at the cruel betrayal of event.

But still you kept faith
with your ideals.
Still you sought out
the highest value of the human being.
Still you believed—
in the character of men and women
who would fill the world
with the brilliant glittering
of jewels and pearls;

that the floral gardens of democracy
would continue to spread.

You lived true to your words:
"Liberty, let others despair of you—
I never despair of you."

Fanfare of flight
performed by a soul erupting
from the abyss of pain!

The poet sets sail
on the journey home
across the spirit's great and fertile sea—
toward the eternal, the essential source
that extends behind all nature.

Living through turbulence
exuding the bright beams of your love
you never ceased your seeking
for the font of life's light.

Walt Whitman, explorer of the spirit—
you are the friend of my heart!

How can I describe the raptures
inspired in my mind
by this one book of poems
encountered in the midst
of the sufferings of youth!
Leaves of Grass—
the very title echoes with
freshness, beauty and strength.

On that day our dialogue began—
the sheer and solitary
nobility of your spirit
fanned within me flames of courage;
your vision of a light-filled future
brought up surging energy and hope.

The utter overflowing freedom
of your soul
struck me like a bolt
of empathetic lightning—
sundering the dark,
making bright the path of my progress,
inviting me toward the great way
of humanity.

Walt Whitman, giant star of freedom!
It is already one hundred years
since your passing—
but I have been with you.

Like a bird bathed in the sun's light
as it flies through the sky,
like a sailor on a night sea
addressing the stars,
I have spoken with you
of humanity's tomorrow,
sung songs of praise to life,
pondered the laws
that govern the infinite universe.

The curtain is falling
on the twentieth century;

the evening sky is shrouded
with perplexed fog.
But, look closer! Look harder!
In the depths of the thick haze
is the powerfully flowing
current of the age
toward a new dawning
of democracy.

This spiritual tide,
this thirst for freedom,
has borne the assaults
of raging militarism;
it has writhed in the spume;
its progress has been blocked
by stagnant reefs of decadence.

But time has grown to fullness
and the tide now rises;
with the joyous booming of waves
—the exult of ordinary citizens—
it washes all the world's shores.

The democratic ideal you espoused
has survived the trials and selections
of more than a century;
it has been passed on
in the conscience of the people
of countries everywhere;
it cracks open the door
on a new age of democracy,
brilliant and eternal in the night

of an uncharted era
bereft of all philosophy.

Walt Whitman, my friend—
it is just as you believed,
just as you proclaimed:
freedom has never betrayed you
humanity has never betrayed you.

The century's twilight
is prelude to the dawn,
the daybreak of the new age,
the beginning of new hope.

Look! My friend—
I will take up the banners
of democracy and freedom
which you held so proudly aloft;
I will fight on and will advance
along the path of the poet,
pioneer of the spirit's wilderness,
on a journey of infinite mission,
forging paths of friendship
to all corners of the Earth,
joining with people heart to heart
ringing out humanity's victory song.

You live within my breast—
like the sun brimming with
compassion and fight;
the rush of your blood's tide,
the thunderous pulse of your heart

courses hotly through my veins.
Walt Whitman, my sun!
Light my way, shine on forever!

> March 26, 1992
> (pp. 217–26)

DAISAKU IKEDA is widely known as a peace activist, religious leader of the lay Buddhist group Soka Gakkai International, founder of the Soka school system in Japan and of colleges in two nations, and honorary proprietor of a major Japanese newspaper. He is also the author of *The Human Revolution*, a multivolume historical novel about the development of the Soka Gakkai, and *The New Human Revolution* series, which began in 1993 and is currently ongoing. Although poetry is vital in Ikeda's life—he has published poems in periodicals and books for more than four decades—few critics have offered commentary on it. Ronald Bosco, Sarah Wider and I welcome the chance to help initiate that discussion.

I both applaud Ikeda's work as a peace activist and am fascinated by his poetic response to Walt Whitman. My interest in Ikeda's and Whitman's reception in Japan is partly shaped by family history: my grandfather taught economics at the University of Tokyo for thirteen years, from 1908 to 1921, and he witnessed some of the early stages of the rise of a militant Japanese nationalism when he visited Korea, then under the control of Japan. My grandfather died unexpectedly in an accident, leaving behind a widow and her six-month-old son, my father.

My father and grandmother left Japan shortly thereafter, but my father's life was intertwined with Japan again when, during World War II, he was drawn into the United States Marine Corps and served as a medic on the front lines, surviving the Pacific battles of Guam and Okinawa, among others. Perhaps in some indirect way, my father's experience as a medic drew me to the writings of Walt Whitman and, in particular, his American Civil War writings recounting his devotion to wounded soldiers.

Whitman and Ikeda both made efforts to offset the destructiveness of war. In the Civil War hospitals of Washington, D. C., Whitman dedicated himself to easing pain, promoting healing and—through attentiveness, small kindnesses and love—saving as many lives as possible. As we know, the Civil War was the bloodiest conflict in the history of the United States, costing perhaps 620,000 lives over the course of five years and extending over American soil from Texas to Pennsylvania. Although sectional bitterness and hatred ran high in the Civil War, Whitman tended to northern and southern soldiers, blacks and whites. For Ikeda, Whitman's love for the common man on both sides in the Civil War is memorable and moving:

> Ah, your noble altruism!
> In the agonized vortex
> of the Civil War
> you rushed from place to place
> nursing the wounded
> equally, without distinction between
> the soldiers of the North
> and those of the South.

The ability to love even one's enemies—always an unusual trait—was manifested in Whitman's life just as it is seen in Ikeda's generous response to American thinkers and culture.

Ikeda's deep interest in American writers—especially the nineteenth-century transcendentalists like Whitman, Ralph Waldo Emerson and Henry David Thoreau, who combined spiritualism with nature poetry in the context of national self-definition—is striking since it emerges so soon after Japanese-American conflict in World War II. Ikeda and his family faced devastation from recurrent B-29 raids starting in 1944:

> My hometown of Kamata had been engulfed in a great conflagration, cruel as hell itself, and was reduced to ashes. My family had to relocate from our home in Kojiya under government orders. We were to stay with an aunt in Magome, but just as we had finished moving, the house in Magome suffered a direct hit by an incendiary bomb during a major air raid on May 24[, 1945]. We had no choice but to live in a rough shack with a tin roof that we built on top of the burned-out site.[1]

Ikeda, however, does not place blame on the American bombers: "The flames with which Japan had burned China and other countries of Asia and the South Pacific had returned to devour Japan."[2]

Ikeda, the fifth son of a seaweed farmer, was too young (and too ill with tuberculosis) for active military service, though he worked in the Niigata Steelworks beginning in 1942 as part of a youth labor corps. Ikeda and his family felt the full effect of war:

> Our family saw
> my four elder brothers,
> all in the prime of life,
> called away to war.
> All four were made tools
> of Japan's invasion of China.
> My eldest brother
> was sent to fight in Burma,
> where he died in battle.
> ("August 15—The dawn of a new day," p. 342)

Ikeda's brothers who survived the war came back stunned, transformed, lost. When Ikeda speaks of the "scorched ruins" out of which his poetic career began, he speaks literally rather than metaphorically. Given the nature of wartime propaganda, his ultimate embrace of an international outlook was quite remarkable.

> None of us had wanted
> this war.
> We had never
> accepted or supported it.
>
> Yet over time
> almost without noticing,
> we were all influenced,
> maneuvered and brainwashed
> to extol the glories of war.
> ("August 15—The dawn of a new day," p. 344)

But Ikeda is selective in what he embraces in American culture; none of the writers he is most influenced by (Emerson, Thoreau and Whitman) rely heavily on Christian language and imagery, and they all positioned themselves as in some ways outsiders from the mainstream of American society.

Though Ikeda did not personally fight in World War II, its battles, particularly those on Okinawa, are nonetheless key to his thought and perhaps to his connection to Whitman in particular. The Battle of Okinawa was arguably more intensely horrific than the American Civil War: in a much more confined area and in only three months, 240,000 people died. That is, more than one-third as many people died in one-twentieth of the time. The last line of defense for Japan in the war, Okinawa became, in Ikeda's words in the 1988 poem "Be an eternal bastion of peace" (pp. 147–67), "a sacrificial pawn / in the defense of the Japanese mainland."

The local people were deemed to be expendable and suffered grievously.

For Japanese, Americans and Okinawans the main island of Okinawa became a black hole of death—a temporally and geographically condensed human catastrophe. Ikeda's message of peace thus emerges both out of the wartime imprisonment of his predecessors Tsunesaburo Makiguchi and Josei Toda—the first and second presidents of the Soka Gakkai and opponents of Japanese militarism; Makiguchi died from malnutrition and abuse suffered in prison—and out of the ashes of World War II itself. Though Ikeda's peacemaking efforts often focus on memorializing Hiroshima's and Nagasaki's devastation and renewal, because of the scale and drama of the atomic bomb, he sees Okinawa as sharing with these sites the "most unspeakable horrors of war." Ikeda underlines the irony of Okinawa, often a haven for sailors, becoming a place marked by violence and trauma:

> Unflinching in your love of peace,
> deeply loyal in friendship,
> kindhearted,
> you rescued and nourished
> untold numbers of foreign friends
> who came shipwrecked
> to your shores.

But what Ikeda calls the "muddy currents of history / swept down upon / these lovely coral islands." At a crossroads in the Pacific, Okinawans have regularly been at the mercy of more powerful forces. Japan and Okinawa are half-brothers, as it were, with considerable shared history of economic, social and military achievements, tensions and tragedies. Okinawa resonates for Ikeda because it is and is not Japan; its people are linked to the Japanese mainland yet also distinct from them culturally and ethnically. With purposeful symbolism, Ikeda began writing *The Human Revolution* on Okinawa, and he has made many trips to this blood-saturated and still strategically vital place. At the urging of Ikeda, the dismantled nuclear missile base in the town of Onna was converted into the Okinawa World Peace Monument. Moreover, Ikeda wrote a significant poem on Okinawa, "Be an eternal bastion of peace," again seeking to remake the legacy and future of Okinawa:

> Green mountains and streams
> were stained with blood,
> the agonized cries
> of an earthly hell
> filled the air.
>
> Innocent people fled in terror
> through the flames of war.
> The "Typhoon of Steel"
> raged on without pity.
> Artillery fire destroyed hills,
> pounding and pulverizing the land.
> Flames reached deep
> into trenches and caves,
> incinerating all within—
> soldiers, mothers, students,
> young girls, infants . . .
> People were ordered
> to commit mass suicide.

Ikeda's forceful and unflinching account of horrific experience in these lines departs from his more typical emphasis on hope for the future. His direct treatment of mass suicide is especially important in light of recent efforts to rewrite this history.[3] The frank, no-nonsense and unsentimental style employed here is similar to Whitman's approach to writing about the war in his *Memoranda During the War*, later incorporated into his autobiographical *Specimen Days*. But Ikeda implicates the state in the horrors of war to a greater extent than Whitman did. For Whitman, the criminal mistakes and cruelty of politicians and generals and slave owners were aberrations out of step with the promise and destiny of American democracy. Interestingly, Ikeda's account does not spare the United States:

> Further suffering followed
> in the wake of Japan's defeat,
> as Okinawa became a land
> administered by the United States,
> a land of military bases.
> Over these islands,
> missile batteries
> cast their black shadows.
> From here bombers took off
> for Vietnam.

It is not possible to *explain* Ikeda's entire body of poetry by pointing to just one source or philosophical doctrine, but Whitman, both because of his experience of the devastation of war and afterward his participation in the reconstruction of the United States (half of which was under military occupation) along more egalitarian principles, was one important contributing influence. Ikeda read *Leaves of Grass* soon after World War II, and his account of the experience is illuminating:

> In the years following Japan's defeat, when the country was under the occupation forces, I remember with fondness and gratitude what it meant to me, a poor young man,

to encounter this collection of poems. And when, in the midst of those gray and troubled times, I learned from that book the secret of how to face the future, my initial admiration gave way to intense affection. . . . One time when I was particularly tired I remember flopping down on the grass in the outer garden of the Meiji Shrine, opening my copy of Leaves of Grass, and reading avidly for the better part of an autumn day. Even now there are three yellowed gingko leaves pressed between the pages.[4]

The original building of the Meiji Shrine was destroyed in World War II during the Tokyo air raids, so Ikeda read *Leaves of Grass* in a setting that underscored both destruction and the promise of peace. Gingko trees are famous for their strength and longevity (four gingko trees survived the atomic blast in Hiroshima and are alive today). The tree is known as the "bearer of hope" and a symbol of peace.[5] The gingko has a connection to Buddhism, too, since it came to Japan from China and was planted near temples. Ikeda's reading of *Leaves of Grass* as akin to a sacred text might be described as the ideal response Whitman hoped for from readers. For Ikeda, *Leaves of Grass* was vital, perhaps even transformative:

This book was the companion of my youth. No, it would be better to say that this book *was* my youth, for everything that is necessary to youth—courage, passion, the future—I found in it.[6]

Ikeda's earliest encounter with Whitman seems to have been "Song of the Open Road,"[7] a poem he read at age nineteen and praises highly because it is so "uplifting and positive." Like Whitman, Ikeda is future-oriented (Whitman used the word "yesterday" only once in the entire so-called deathbed edition of *Leaves of Grass*, the most complete compilation of his poems). Ikeda and

Whitman each liked the open road image because both embraced the "boundless possibility" of the future.[8] Mobility is also a key marker of the shift from a feudal/peasant society to one where individuals are "freed" to pursue economic self-interest—slaves can't travel, nor can serfs. Postwar Japan offered a greater degree of liberation to certain classes, and perhaps no individual's development illustrates this more dramatically than Ikeda himself.

In "The Poetry that Touches the Human Spirit: Walt Whitman's *Leaves of Grass*," Ikeda mentions reading Whitman again when he was twenty-two (1950) in a translation done by Saika Tomita, though elsewhere he suggests he was twenty-three.[9] In either case, it would have been early in his career, at a time when he was employed by Okura Shoji, one of the business ventures of his mentor, Josei Toda. The first two sentences of "The Poetry that Touches the Human Spirit" both stress Whitman's connection to "ordinary people," making clear Ikeda's admiration of this aspect of *Leaves of Grass*.[10] Ikeda recognizes that Whitman's faith in common humanity fuels his undaunted optimism about democracy and strength of spirit in adversity. Ikeda also notes that Whitman was as "strong as a weed" (Ikeda's poem opening this essay says the roots of the common people are like weeds) and describes himself in a charmingly self-deprecatory way as a weed here:

> Rather than live as a
> brief and high-minded flower,
> I want to live
> a weed-like life
> of tenacious vitality.
> (*"To my young friends," p. 24*)

Ikeda's own admiration for ordinary people, his sense of the glorious quality of features others might find homely, is also apparent in "Treasures":

I also treasure
A young man's glistening eyes,
The teenager's soiled overalls,
The farmer's gnarled hands,
A grandmother's selfless wrinkles,
   melting into smiles.[11]

Part of Ikeda and Whitman's ability to identify with the common and tenacious rather than the rare and delicate involved a reappraisal of the merits of ordinary people. Whitman admired the courage and stoicism of the least recognized soldiers who endured the consequences of battle, those whose deeds were invisible in conventional histories, but whose sacrifices and achievements validated his faith in democracy. In parts of *Leaves of Grass*, he indicates that the spirit of democratic revolution has to be reborn through each new generation's struggles. Ikeda, though a pacifist, similarly calls on martial metaphors in his quest for peace through a more democratic society, arguing that "we advance / in the sincere and bloodless battle of the century."[12] Ikeda speaks regularly of victory of this kind in militant terms:

The pitched battles
in which youth engage
will invariably bring down
every last adversary of the Buddha.
(*"Unfurl the banner of youth,"* p. 262)

Does victory, for him and for his followers, imply defeat for someone else? One explanation is that he seems to engage in thinking that is beyond rational, thinking that is akin to Whitman's belief in the possibility of "unnumbered Supremes" and in the "divine average."[13] But it also may imply a defeat for those who have invested in an older and more hierarchical order for society.

In his personal poetry, Ikeda's use of martial imagery is again striking. We could regard this as a contradiction for a pacifist, but it is better understood as a paradox. Ikeda is not naïve about the world and the struggles within it. Martial language offers a way to signal the intensity of the effort and struggle needed to create change.

> A proud and independent champion,
> I wait for no one.
> My heart is the site of ceaseless struggle,
> a battlefield where fierce contests are waged—
> the advance and retreat
> of hope and despair,
> courage and cowardice,
> progress and stagnation.
> ("*Unfurl the banner of youth*," p. 260)

In the passage above, the "I" or persona created by Ikeda acknowledges warring elements within the self, perhaps paralleling spiritual struggle with the concentrated focus needed for aiding people more broadly. Whitman does not use quite these terms; when he turns inwards to the spirit, his poetry simultaneously explores the mysteries, anguish and joys of the body and human sexuality.

In Ikeda's "Preface" to his collection of poems *Hopes and Dreams*, he invokes Whitman in the first paragraph: "Ever since I was a boy I have been fond of poetry, finding particular enjoyment in reading Walt Whitman in translation or Japanese poets like Doi Bansui." He goes on to say, "Because my verse is so private, the mere thought of presenting it to the public and thus exposing myself to embarrassment is a source of discomfort."[14] Perhaps we should understand this as a standard disclaimer—an almost obligatory statement of proper modesty. Whitman's influence here is indirect; Whitman wrote a poem called "Song of Myself" that similarly seemed to promise revelation of his personal life but instead and with great audacity expanded that "self" to include people of all types.

Ikeda's poetry is private because it is personal and heartfelt, but to American readers his writings will not seem like the confessional poetry of, say, John Berryman, Sylvia Plath, Robert Lowell, Anne Sexton or others who probed the inner (and sometimes tortured) workings of the mind. In contrast, Ikeda's interest is not in portraying anguish, self-doubt and psychological complexities: inner turmoil, when mentioned, tends to be tamed and overcome, perhaps because he is always conscious of his role as a spiritual, social and educational leader. When he does talk about inner struggles or failings, it is in a generalized or philosophical way as in the final lines of "I offer this to you" (p. 12):

> It is good to struggle.
> Because unless we pass
> through the dark depths of night
> we cannot greet
> the noble dignity
> of the dawn.

Like Whitman, Ikeda's writing here and elsewhere avoids dense allusiveness. Sometimes Ikeda's verse also lacks the striking image or unusual turn of phrase that can bring a personal experience vividly to life, though in war poems the seemingly cooler and blander style functions effectively in contrast to the horrors being described. That said, his poems on spiritual warfare are accessible and deeply valued, especially by his followers, for their inspirational quality and optimism, and perhaps for their very attentiveness to the private or interior struggles of the self. Though Whitman in his own day wrote of "the self" in a free verse that surprised readers by its innovations, for twentieth- and twenty-first-century audiences aware of the rich but often obscure language of modern poets, Whitman's style would seem surprisingly simple and clear. Ikeda suggests he follows a similar strategy or is part of an international tradition of writing in a plain style:

> I do not write for the critic. My sole intentions are to express forthrightly the feelings that come to me in the context of my daily life and activities, and to convey my hopes for the future. It may sound radical, but I wonder if poetry is not the free expression of such feelings and hopes? The poetry of the *Manyoshu* has survived over a thousand years and continues to throb with life; Whitman's *Leaves of Grass* continues to transcend national boundaries as it powerfully exalts the cries of the individual.[15]

Ikeda sees this approach—he does not write for the *literati*, who in Japanese history had ties to the aristocracy—as being similar in important ways to Whitman of whom he said: "You do not sing to please the critics." Whitman himself seemed to desire that the reader be a brother, someone who embraced his ideas and feelings, rather than a critic attuned to style or form.

Ikeda first encountered Whitman in a period when avant-garde poetry, with its often elliptical phrasing, was increasingly marginalized in American newspapers and popular culture. Ikeda understands Whitman as a forefather of experimentation with poetic language and identifies this freedom as key to the lasting power of the *Manyoshu*, the oldest extant collection of Japanese poetry, and *Leaves of Grass*:

> In both cases the poetry is alive and meaningful today because it reveals the human spirit and relates to what is basically human—to that which cannot be captured merely by the pedantry of poetic form and convention.[16]

Ikeda acknowledges that "it may seem presumptuous to mention great works like the *Manyoshu* and *Leaves of Grass* in the same breath as amateurish verse," but he explains that his purpose is to suggest the proper framework for evaluating his poetry:

> I would be happy if people see that my feelings resonate more directly with the relatively free and democratic verse of the *Manyoshu* (mid-eighth century) than with the disciplined and aristocratic *waka* of the *Kokinshu* (early tenth century), more with Walt Whitman than with John Keats.[17]

Despite Ikeda's affinity with Whitman, and with realism over self-conscious art, he is more didactic than the poet of *Leaves of Grass*: "I know of no greater joy therefore than to imagine that even one line or one phrase of my verse might somehow touch the reader's heart and awaken him to life by indicating what to strive for and how to live."[18] Whitman, too, wished to awaken the reader, but he hoped to do so more indirectly by promoting an awareness of the interrelated sanctity of both body and soul, trusting his readers to follow more readily via suggestion than direct instruction. For Whitman, insight and physicality were inextricably intertwined. He wanted to be in direct contact with the reader:

> Camerado, this is no book,
> Who touches this touches a man,
> (Is it night? are we here together alone?)
> It is I you hold and who holds you,
> I spring from the pages into your arms.[19]

Whitman wanted to "pass"—from poet to reader, from one identity to another, from his time to later generations—and it is through an intimate voice that he reimagines the very act of reading, making it a bodily, at times even carnal experience. And yet in other moods Whitman was less confident about his ability to convey personal presence. In lines published in the first edition of *Leaves of Grass* but later deleted, he declared:

> This is unfinished business with me . . . . how is it with you?
> I was chilled with the cold types and cylinder and wet paper between us.
>
> I pass so poorly with paper and types . . . . I must pass with the contact of bodies and souls.[20]

Given his desire to have a book perform in such an extraordinary way, Whitman constantly strove to exploit and expand the capacity of print as a medium, even as he chafed against its limitations.

For Ikeda, perhaps because of this idea of intangible touch bringing readers to life, Whitman is frequently associated with the sun. He notes with pleasure that Emerson called Whitman's work a "sunbeam."[21] And in "A Book," Ikeda notes that in reading *Leaves of Grass* he has had the "feeling of a primitive sun whose clear and powerful beams pierce the dense cloud cover to shine upon the earth. These poems have warmed me and given me confidence in the mission I pursue today."[22]

Recurrently, the sun is invoked by Ikeda in discussing Whitman; Ikeda thus absorbs him and appropriates him in a way in keeping with elemental Japanese symbolism and its stress on the sun. The rising sun flag is, of course, unavoidably associated with nationalism and the history of conquest and occupation of East Asia during the war in the Pacific, but Ikeda never wishes to avoid this history but rather to confront, understand and remake it. He links the sun with victory and triumph, but his notion of victory is very different than earlier notions of victory as conquest. Ikeda turns to the sun for brightness, brilliance, illumination and, ultimately, peace.

Ikeda's poem written on the centenary of Whitman's death begins with sun imagery:

> Like the sun rising
> shattering the dark
> of old restraints—
> with new words, new forms
> the soul's liberator
> lauds a new world, a new humanity;
> sings out democracy's dawn.

Later he says: "You live within my breast— / like the sun brimming with / compassion and fight." Like so many other poets and thinkers who have responded to Whitman, Ikeda finds the poet to be a vital force, a continuing presence, an interlocutor able to defy time and dissolution. Ikeda, a great proponent of dialogue, speaks fittingly of the dialogue that began with his first reading of Whitman and continues to this day.

In 1987, Ikeda's poem "Arise, the sun of the century" (pp. 94–104) appeared on the "thirtieth anniversary of the kosen-rufu movement in America." By "kosen-rufu" Ikeda means the ongoing effort to enhance human dignity and to strive toward world peace. Ikeda notes in it that "Since my youth, years ago, / Emerson and Whitman have been my constant companions." He praises the United States as "the great land of freedom" but passes over the fact that it has also been a land of enslavement. Later in the poem, Ikeda adds complexity and acknowledges less pleasant "anxieties." Yet he remains hopeful for the movement's prospects and perhaps by extension, for America's:

> The limitlessness of freedom,
> the rhythms of harmonious collaboration,
> the richness of democratic experience

and the refreshing spirit of pioneering;
the conviction in autonomy,
the unbounded space,
and the vitality of the people united.

It is not clear in remarks such as these whether Ikeda thinks he is describing an actual United States or one he would like to imagine. But in either case there is no shortage of a belief in the transformative potential of the movement. It will produce nothing less than a "new history of America":

In order to create a new American history,
my dear friends,
resolve to be people of trustworthiness.

. . . .

You are the Minutemen of the Mystic Law,[23]
the Whitmans of kosen-rufu,
shouldering the responsibility
to ensure the development
of the next chapter of worldwide kosen-rufu.

Ikeda's desire in this and other poems to instruct readers, to effect change, to influence the lives of particular audiences, sets him apart from many poets from the Romantic era forward, who wrote as if unconscious of a listener, confessing feeling in moments of solitude, to paraphrase John Stuart Mill.[24] Ikeda's sense of the proper function of poetry is closer to an older tradition of civic humanism, which understood poetry as a form of rhetoric, and like rhetoric, meant to persuade individuals to pursue the common good. Whitman both broke from and continued this concept. He wrote for an audience, though he did not always know who that audience would be ("you, whoever you are"), and his poetry was not mimetic in a conventional rhetorical fashion but nevertheless tried for directness and immediacy that would be persuasive and convincing. Ikeda typically addresses an audience, often a highly particular one, whether it is an individual or a group, but in doing so introduces a greater sense of distance between himself as the speaker and adviser and the listener in search of inspiration.

One translator, Robert Epp, notes that Ikeda writes as a "busy workingman to busy workingmen, even to girls and boys. His tone is one of joy and victory, not of sadness and loss."[25] While these poems are no doubt deeply felt, there is a decorousness in the tone of the poems—at least as various translators have rendered him— that maintains a reserve and that keeps the reader at a remove from the marrow of experience. If Ikeda's upbeat tone is regarded as predictable or unearned, it will be seen as a limitation in his poetry. Yet, Ikeda never thinks of himself solely as a poet, and his optimism is a key to his success as a leader of the Soka Gakkai. Whitman, too, we should remember, has been blamed for excessive optimism. And Whitman also believed in the beneficial effects of buoyancy and good cheer as is clear from his description of his preparations for hospital visits.

Robert Epp has argued that Ikeda writes poetry of social "commitment rather than of aesthetic sensibility." Yet he believes that Ikeda "can admire a poet like Whitman whose verse he says 'powerfully exalts the cries of the individual.'"[26] Ikeda, in one of his most socially didactic poems, invokes Whitman this way, saying:

> Walt Whitman writes:
> > O soul, repressless, I with thee and thou with me,
> > Thy circumnavigation of the world begin,
> > Of man, the voyage of his mind's return,
> > To reason's early paradise . . .

> How profound and strong our karmic ties!
> For we also are aware
> of what the great poet sought:
> the early paradise
> is nothing but the Buddha land
> that knows no decline;
> it is nothing but the treasure land
> that knows no dissolution.

He and Whitman are after the same goal—democracy that permits common humanity to flourish: "'the carpenter singing his (song) as he measures his plank or beam,' . . . These are, after all, the basic concerns of Daisaku Ikeda, too."[27]

The poem "The sun of jiyu over a new land" (pp. 236–49) was written to commemorate the second general meeting of the Soka Gakkai International-USA. It is artful in its blending of optimism about Los Angeles being a city of the world's future and a place with deep problems. Ikeda was writing in the shadow of the Rodney King riots sparked by the acquittal of several policemen involved in the vicious beating of an African American. (The beating was captured on video and created outrage far and wide.) Ikeda's hopes for the SGI in the United States and for Soka University of America were tied up with California as illustrating America's promise as a place of international mixing ("There is no question that / your multiracial nation, America, / represents humanity's future"). But the United States has lingering and severe racial problems. Significantly, he turns to Whitman near the end of the poem:

> Walt Whitman
> giant of the American Renaissance
> penned these words:
> "Come, I will make the continent indissoluble,
> I will make the most splendid race the sun ever shone upon,

> I will make divine magnetic lands,
>   With the love of comrades,
>   With the life-long love of comrades."

Ah, Los Angeles!

People appropriate Whitman in various ways and turn him to their purposes. Ikeda acknowledged Whitman's more obvious connections with Japan in several ways. He appreciated Whitman's interest in Eastern religions and applauded Whitman's poem "A Broadway Pageant" (first published as "The Errand Bearers"), which treats Japan's inaugural appearance on the stage of international diplomacy. Ikeda paid Whitman's expansiveness a more profound compliment when he said: "Thinking of Whitman's poetic cosmos reminds me of the Buddhist scriptures. The canon is immense and took ages to build."[28] But it seems clear that it is the international Whitman of comrades and the divine average of all races—the poet of democracy—that is most influential for Ikeda.

Ikeda's poem on Whitman, "Like the sun rising," shows a good understanding of his reception, including the early reviews that he quotes in the poem, underlining the critics' displeasure at the freedom Whitman permitted himself and, by extension, the ordinary citizen. Whitman's example may have encouraged Ikeda to write and behave in iconoclastic ways, too. Ikeda argues that he advances the cause of Whitman, taking up the "banners / of democracy and freedom / which you held so proudly aloft." The claim is bold, even audacious. On a political level, and to some extent on a poetic one as well, he has tried to fulfill this promise. With justice, he sees himself as in harmony with his key American predecessors and "the world of which / Emerson, Whitman and Thoreau dreamed." For Ikeda, they show the "path humanity must pursue" in our time ("The triumph of the human spirit," p. 377).

Notes

1. Daisaku Ikeda, *The World Is Yours to Change* (Tokyo: Asahi Shuppansha, 2002), p. 191.
2. Ibid.
3. Masaaki Aniya, "Compulsory Mass Suicide, the Battle of Okinawa, and Japan's Textbook Controversy," *The Okinawa Times* and *Asahi Shimbun*, *The Asia-Pacific Journal: Japan Focus* website: http://www.japanfocus.org/-Aniya-Masaaki/2629 (accessed August 15, 2013).
4. Daisaku Ikeda, "A Book," in *Glass Children and Other Essays*, Burton Watson, trans. (Tokyo and New York: Kodansha International, 1979), p. 41.
5. This information is drawn from the website of the Japanese American National Museum. http://janmstore.com/ginkgo.html (accessed July 31, 2013).
6. Ikeda, *Glass Children*, p. 41.
7. Daisaku Ikeda, "Dialogue for the Future: Traveling the Path of Victory Together With You," *World Tribune*, June 1, 2012, p. 5.
8. Ibid.
9. Daisaku Ikeda, "The Poetry that Touches the Human Spirit: Walt Whitman's *Leaves of Grass*," *Living Buddhism* 10 (January/February 2006), p. 90. Also, Ikeda, *Glass Children*, p. 39.
10. Ikeda, "The Poetry that Touches the Human Spirit," p. 92.
11. Daisaku Ikeda, "Treasures" in *Hopes and Dreams,* Robert Epp, trans. (Santa Monica, Calif.: World Tribune Press, 1976), p. 54.
12. Ikeda, "Song of Youth" in *Songs from My Heart*, Burton Watson, trans. (New York and Tokyo, Weatherhill, 1978), p. 14.
13. Walt Whitman, *Leaves of Grass* (Brooklyn: n.p., 1855), p. vii; and Whitman, *Leaves of Grass* (Boston: Thayer and Eldridge, 1860), p. 194. Both are available on *The Walt Whitman Archive* (whitmanarchive.org).
14. Ikeda, "Preface," in *Hopes and Dreams*, p. 11.
15. Ibid., p. 12.
16. Ibid.
17. Ibid.
18. Ibid.
19. Walt Whitman, *Leaves of Grass* (Philadelphia: David McKay, 1891), p. 382. Available on *The Walt Whitman Archive* (whitmanarchive.org).
20. Whitman, *Leaves of Grass* (Brooklyn: n.p., 1855), p. 57.
21. Ikeda, "The Poetry that Touches the Human Spirit," p. 92.

22. Ikeda, *Glass Children*, p. 41.
23. The poetry frequently invokes the Mystic Law, a term that could be defined as "life force of the universe."
24. John Stuart Mill, *Dissertations and Discussions: Political, Philosophical, and Historical*, vol. 1 (London: Longman, Green, Reader, and Dyer, 1875), p. 71.
25. Robert Epp, "Translator's Note" in Ikeda, *Hopes and Dreams*, p. 7.
26. Ibid., pp. 7, 9.
27. Ibid., p. 9.
28. Ikeda in Ronald A. Bosco, Joel Myerson and Daisaku Ikeda, *Creating Waldens: An East–West Conversation on the American Renaissance* (Cambridge, Mass.: Dialogue Path Press, 2009), p. 125. Originally published in Japanese: *Utsukushiki seimei—chikyu to ikiru* (Tokyo: Mainichi Shimbun, 2006).

Daisaku Ikeda's Poetry of Encouragement

SARAH ANN WIDER

PREFACE

MAY THE FRAGRANT LAURELS OF HAPPINESS ADORN YOUR LIFE

Dedicated to my beloved young women's division members

How beautiful is the sun,
its limitless, multihued lights revealing
the inherent dignity of humankind!
This undeniable force,
this unfaltering existence dedicated
to fulfilling its vow,
to illuminating all things for all time!

In the presence of the sun
there is no darkness.
In the presence of the sun
there is no discrimination.
In the presence of the sun
the same rights are shared by all

and a world of peace shines brightly.

Today once more
I will walk my chosen path
pursue my chosen work
bring my history to new luster.
Undeterred by deceitful rains,
I will walk a path of bright smiles
true to myself, as only I can,
undefeated by anything!
For I understand this path
to be my treasured way.

Youth—
this time in life that comes but once,
dignified and precious
like a glittering gem.
I will live vivaciously, with all my might.
Because to do so is to lay the foundations
of a lifetime,
and from here is born a new happiness
arising from the very core of my being.

I will never stop advancing!
Even in the face of great difficulties
I will not turn back.
Life must be lived—
strongly, honestly, cheerfully!

Of course there will be bad times
along with the good.
But I will never hurl insults at life.

The growing vital force that is youth—
in each joyous stride
there is so much to read and learn
so much wisdom to seek.

Whatever the blizzards of this life
you can emerge triumphant
by the strengths residing
within your heart.

What a joyful prospect—
to live each day of youth
with wisdom, savoring happiness
and meaningful hope
in a world peopled with beautiful hearts!

In such a life,
everything you undergo
forms a fragrant crown
of woven flowers
that adorns your brow.

Daughter of unfathomable mission!
You transform the ashen winter landscape
into a vivid dance of spring
bathed in soft sunlight.

I will not lose my footing
in the morass of society.
I feel no envy for the illusory shadows
of glamour and fame.
Nor am I shaken by heartless criticism.

For I embrace principles
that are eternal
and merit my complete faith.
I have my SGI family—
sisters who share my aspirations,
who are trustworthy
and with whom I can share anything.

The inner vitality of youth
bright as the morning sun
holds all the world's wealth of gold.
To be young, in itself,
is to inhabit a castle of jewels.

The palace of your life sparkles
with the light of gems more numerous
than the stars filling the heavens.

Nothing could be more sublime
than this treasure possessed by all.
No one in this world is better than others.
We are all equally, ordinarily human.

In his later years
the world-acclaimed violinist
Yehudi Menuhin declared:
God resides within our hearts.
Likewise, the Buddha is found
within our lives,
not in temples or monasteries.

This treasure is something

that no one can take from you
for it *is* you, you yourself.
To awaken to this fact
is happiness.

Just as the lamp you light for another
will illuminate your own way,
the heart that desires the happiness of others
will be filled with the bright starlight
of happiness.

My joy is not confined
within a narrow room.
There is space for all to enter,
for this friend and that.

The forces of selfish ego
work to drive others out,
to gain sole possession
of the jeweled chamber.
Such people end up
banished from their own palace,
left to wander in hellish solitude.

The warm camaraderie
of friends joined hand in hand,
like endless vistas of floral garlands,
multiplies my joy many times over.

"Kindness is the flower of strength,"
said José Martí, hero of Cuban independence.

As a flower that blooms proudly
despite the pelting rains,
I will share this smile
with my friends and companions!

If you are cowardly or weak
you cannot offer others protection.
In the end, you'll be left facing
your most pitiable, compassionless self.

Only by triumphing over your own sorrow
can you fully feel the dark misery
afflicting a friend.
Only when you win over your own weakness
can you ease the troubles of others.

Be strong! Ever strong!
These are the crucial watchwords
that open the doors
to the palace of happiness.
Bid farewell to songs of sadness.
Triumph over inner weakness.
Reject self-deception
and come to know yourself
as someone who never betrays
what is true and just!

Faith is not emotionalism or self-pity;
it is about winning in your life!

Daughter with sparkling eyes!
Your youth alone makes you
a princess of happiness!
Soar high above the

sinister anguished clouds!
Stretch wide the wings of freedom
propelled by the vibrant force
of your spirit!
Gaze down from those heights
on festering swamps of envy!

You must never submit
to forlornly swaying emotions.
Maintain your pride and dignity!
Direct your heart with
firmness and certainty!

Always remember
you are a monarch of humanity!
Maintain regal focus
on a treasured throne
enveloped in a world
of rich colors and varied lights!

Nichiren Daishonin instructs us
to be the masters of our minds
and not let our minds be our masters.
These words are an eternal beacon
to light your life's journey.

In my heart—
the flame of an imperishable philosophy burns
the light of lifetime purpose shines
magnificent goals reside.

Those whose hearts are set
on profound and focused prayer
are freed from hesitancy.

They do not fear
the aimless drifting into darkness.
In the depths of their being
a bright, untrammeled path
of peace and contentment
unfolds without end.

I will not drown in the
illusory images of renown
as they shimmer fleetingly
on the water's surface!

Make companions
of the sun and the moon
as they shine with undying light!
Take joy in quiet striving
on the ground of daily living.
Live out your life in its actuality
—in the midst of reality—
advancing always toward happiness!

Noble young women!
Do not cling to trivial things!
For the foolish find themselves living
far from the realm of heavenly beings.
They will be carried off by angry, roaring waves.

Never be deceived or taken in!
There is not the slightest need
to be jealous
of anyone else!

Only you know the reality

of your own life.
The scorn of others
based on their personal perception
is nothing more than that.
Live true to yourself—
those who do
are happy.

If you are wise and clear-sighted
you have already attained
a life of magnificent victory.

I possess the mirror
of pristine life
that reflects with unsparing clarity
the evil of this world—
a life that, like the pure white lotus,
remains unsullied
amidst the dirt and dust
of a squalid age!
I possess the jewel-encrusted
sword of an idealism that makes
the corrupt and unscrupulous
tremble in shame!

Fresh new flower of revolution!
Joan of Arc for the coming era!
With your silvery voice
you reinvigorate
the sleepy veterans
of past campaigns;
you inspire courage in the hearts
of a fatigued generation

spurring them
to rise and fight again.

History recounts
that Joan of Arc
was just an ordinary girl.
But the people of the village
where she lived described her
as a young woman of initiative.

She willingly worked,
she readily spun,
she gladly pulled the plow . . .
And when the time came,
she took the lead
to fight and rescue
France from peril!

The curtain is now rising
on the grand stage
of the twenty-first century!
The time has come
for the daughters of the sun
crowned with laurels
to take the lead
to move with vibrant
grace and courage!

A fresh breeze blows
and the pure blue sky
stretches into eternity.
So let us spread our wings!

Rise dancing bravely into the sky,
fly with flaming hope
into the future that awaits
in the vast new century
that is yours.

Daughters of the sun!
Always remember
the noble mothers and fathers
who worked selflessly
braving wind and rain
to build this Soka castle
of value creation!

 March 24, 1999
 (pp. 268–76)

  Become strong!
  Become strong!
  Become strong without fail![1]

WHAT DO YOU MAKE of those words? Where does your mind travel as you read? What journey does your memory take? Have you encountered the words before? When? Are they an affirmation of what is innate? A call to create what does not yet exist? Who is the speaker? Who, the listener? Is this a welcome imperative? An impossible command? What pulse rests in the rhythm of the words themselves? It evokes a beating heart, but what heart is this?

 I open with questions and uncertainty, the place where dialogue most fruitfully begins. This evocative place is central to Daisaku Ikeda's lifework, whether in education, nuclear disarmament, environmental justice or poetry. One could well say that "poetry" comprehends the whole, that Ikeda's lifelong commitment to building cultures of peace while actively opposing cultures of violence is fundamentally rooted in a poetic understanding of the world.

"Cosmic rhythms and ingenious nature": The poet at work

In a dialogue with David Krieger, founder of the Nuclear Age Peace Foundation, Ikeda raises the fundamental connection between poetry and action. Poetry is as poetry does. He comments,

> Poetry manifests the human spirit; it is an artistic expression of faith, an irrepressible outflowing of the human soul with energy to move the minds of others. Superior poetic words lift the reader's spirit, inspiring reverence, for cosmic rhythms and ingenuous nature. Poetry can also be a call to resist oppression. The hearts of poets, embodied in their words, arouse sympathetic vibrations in readers' minds.[2]

I quote the passage in full to launch our dialogue with Ikeda's poetry as well as with our own understandings of poetry.

Consider the constellation of thought he presents. The sentences are marked by activity. Poetry "manifests," "lifts," "inspires," "calls," "arouses." It is characterized by "irrepressible outflowing" and "the energy to move minds." The latter is a singular ability. How immovable the human mind can be. For Ikeda, poetry is the force by which mired minds can once again take flight, or at least begin to walk. Little wonder, then, that poetry actively resists oppression. He explains this using a musical metaphor grounded in the reality of the physical human being. For those of us who have lived in musical homes or workplaces, we know the phenomenon well. You are sitting at your instrument, not playing, though someone nearby is. Suddenly your instrument is also vibrating, whether the strings or the wood. My favorite memory comes from a performance of *Symphonie Fantastique* by Hector Berlioz where the very stage on which we were performing vibrated with our sound, becoming the immense sounding board for the piece. When you listen to music and feel those vibrations in your gut, it is not only your imagination at work. Given the physical properties of sound waves and the vibratory properties of matter, there are frequent confluences between the source of sound and what is close at hand. Ikeda uses this physical law, allying it with the "cosmic rhythms and ingenious nature" to describe the effect of a poet's work on a reader's mind. That sympathetic vibration aroused in the reader in turn enables the reader not only to perceive oppression but also irreversibly feel its injustice and understand its urgency.

As poet Audre Lorde wrote in 1977 in her essay of the same title, "Poetry is Not a Luxury." Reversing the all-too-common contemporary American expectation that poetry either belongs to an elite group of people or that poetry means rhymes for childhood and is thereby something we grow out of, Lorde calls attention to the essential connection between poetry and change. Writing within the context of black women's oppression, she challenges the limitations placed on poetry:

> I speak here of poetry as a revelatory distillation of experience, not the sterile word play that, too often, the white fathers distorted the word *poetry* to mean—in order to cover a desperate wish for imagination without insight.
>
> For women, then, poetry is not a luxury. It is a vital necessity of our existence. It forms the quality of the light within which we predicate our hopes and dreams toward survival and change, first made into language, then into idea, then

into more tangible action. Poetry is the way we help give name to the nameless so it can be thought. The farthest horizons of our hopes and fears are cobbled by our poems, carved from the rock experiences of our daily lives.[3]

Lorde's understanding of poetry highlights the very condition of one's perception. Poetry is the "quality of light" by which we see. That quality in turn shapes what we can imagine in our lives, whether we will have to live someone else's daily lies or realize "survival and change." Within that "quality of light," poetry functions as the necessary catalyst. It makes it possible to say what has not yet been said, to bring into language transformative thought: "first made into language, then into idea, then into more tangible action."

In his dialogues and in his poems, Ikeda addresses what Lorde calls this "vital necessity of our existence." Later in the essay, I will speak further about its singular importance for Japanese women in the Soka Gakkai community, but I turn first to Ikeda's equation of poetry and agency. In his "Salute to poets" (pp. 389–95), written for the twenty-seventh World Congress of Poets, he associates poetry with renewal or perhaps with what is distinctly new. The poem begins:

> There is a power in words,
> an infinite power
> to revive, restore
> and make life blaze anew.
>
> There is a life in poetry,
> a limitless, eternal life
> that can stir and arouse
> a society to new vibrancy.

At first it appears that the stanzas echo each other, substituting "life" for "power" and "poetry" for "words." At closer consideration, the difference in the last line speaks volumes. This is not simply a work of "restoration" but creation: society experiences "new vibrancy." The poem, however, sounds a cautionary note. Verbal power is readily corrupted. It can become a "lethal blade" aimed at division. Words become tools for cutting rather than weaving, for rejecting what is different from oneself rather than inquiring into what we can learn from what we are not.

Ikeda describes this denigration of language as an overpowering flood that leaves people awash in self and in a societally destructive distrust. When the words most commonly heard are "deceptive, vacuous / and violent," listeners come to suspect language itself. Such innate distrust of language cripples the human being. As Ikeda says, "Words are / the human heart." Alienated from the very essence of the self, the individual is indeed divided against him- or herself. There is nothing to trust if words by their very nature are untrustworthy. Ikeda paints a bleak picture that may well ring true for many of us in this particularly contentious and divisive age:

> This flood
> of deceptive, vacuous
> and violent language
> has caused people
> to treat all words and language
> as suspect.
> Words are
> the human heart
> and this doubt
> has driven people
> into the dark and rampant isolation
> of cynicism and fear,
> distrusting everything

including society
and humanity itself.

What happens in a state of such profound distrust? Considering the violence of the early twenty-first century, the effects are all too apparent. Suspicion holds the upper hand. Language is increasingly seen as a means for manipulation. Language becomes defensive; in essence every word does violence. Words are another form of self-defense designed to protect the individual who is supposedly inviolate in isolation.

Here indeed is a world of "imagination without insight." For any life, continuous isolation results in death. For any life, sustained distrust ends in destruction, whether turned inward toward the self or outward toward others. In such straits, it might seem impossible for language to regain its users' trust. Ikeda, however, proposes a solution—one that the early stanzas set in motion in vivid detail. Beginning in the fourth stanza, he directly addresses poets themselves. He describes the poet's work. No topic is off limits. Neither is any approach. A true poem never sanitizes. Illustrating the poet's power, his conjured images are visually and mentally graphic. Death is imminent for the starving infant. The child who might survive turns to violence in the face of hatred and discrimination, and then, if he is "lucky" enough to survive for a few years more, he is a youth who feels himself so disenfranchised that futility defines him.

Anyone with lingering ideas that poetry speaks from a lofty, unearthly ideal soon sees the impossibility in that assumption. Poets "feel the full torment / of people's pain," and in turn their words evoke, not the same pain—that indeed would be deception—but a pain that is power. As Ikeda cleverly moves the lines out from the darkness of these descriptions, he reminds his readers—those who consider themselves poets and those who do not—that every problem mentioned is one "caused and created / by human beings." Caused by human beings, they can also be resolved by them. The rest of the poem models such work, both in the poet's careful and considered use of language and also, to borrow Lorde's phrase, through "the quality of the light" by which a person chooses to see difference. Will it be the preoccupation that divides people across chasms or

> the quality that
> enables us
> to learn from each other,
> to complement and fulfill each other,
> to respect and honor each other[?]

In these lines, Ikeda reminds the reader to tend carefully her or his choices because even in something as seemingly innocuous as selecting a word, one creates a cascading effect.

Underlying this call to attentiveness is Ikeda's understanding that all individuals are potential poets precisely because of their humanity. As he says in this poem,

> We are all human beings.
> The poetic spirit
> beats and throbs
> in our veins!

Returning to Ikeda's discussion with David Krieger, I single out his similar affirmation. Here he notes how the "poetic spirit" makes no distinctions based on societal rank or place. It "encourages [all] people . . . to return to their naked humanity."[4] At a time when many question any "universal," Ikeda unapologetically affirms a fundamental humanity that no social construction can overwrite. Whether we agree or not, it gives us pause to see the agency it opens. He comments, "Neither sentimental nor fantastic, [the poetic spirit] embraces and affirms the whole world and all its inhabitants; it imparts the will to remain optimistic and unbending in the face of all hardships."[5] He assures the reader that this affirmation is no retreat from reality: it cannot be chalked up to unexamined feeling (what Lorde might call an "undisciplined attention" to feeling[6]) or to blind imagination. Rather, it enables the individual to undertake the hardest work in the world. Most of us find it far easier to judge and separate than "complement and fulfill." How would our approach change were we able to nonjudgmentally acknowledge *all* the world's inhabitants and not only those with whom we agree or with whom we associate direct benefit? It also provides the sustaining element without which the individual would be worn down. This optimism is no wishful thinking but a profound resolve. It constitutes an active trust that life-affirming creativity survives through every hardship.

Hardship is the operative word. Ikeda makes clear that poets are no strangers to difficulty. Nor is this difficulty unspecified. It is inextricably intertwined with the struggle for justice. Here are a few examples:

> The true poet
> is born of the fight for justice.
> He awakens and arises
> from amongst a
> people in struggle.
> *("The poet—warrior of the spirit," p. 264)*

> You sing with a clear voice
> . . . .
> of the struggle against injustice.
> *("Together holding aloft laurels of the people's poetry," p. 322)*

Yet in the past
and today as well
the history of the people and their struggle
has been bathed in tears of suffering and want

A poet put it this way:
"While ignorance and misery remain on earth
we will never give up our fight!"
("The people," p. 43)

To undo the prejudice of race
to break down the walls of class
to share freedom and equality with the people—
it is for this that you sing
to the last limits of your strength.
("Like the sun rising," p. 220)

In his essay in this volume, Ken Price discusses in greater detail Ikeda's "people's poetry," and its deep connections with Walt Whitman. For now, I draw your attention to a central element within Ikeda's poetic vision: poetry includes everyone. The property of no specialist, it is the human voice. It speaks, shouts, cries, sings unstoppably for justice. Even in descriptions of beauty or evocations of a feeling or renderings of an occasion, that element of justice for all maintains the rhythm beneath Ikeda's words. Otherwise the poem is only partially realized. It is only a pale shadow of what it could be.

As Ikeda envisions it, the transformative element bound into the very nature of the "poetic" is available everywhere, to everyone, at all times. There is no place where poetry does not exist or cannot come into existence. Before considering how his poems for women demonstrate this aspect of "people's poetry," I return to that state of resistance certain readers and writers of poetry feel when poetry and action are united, especially if that action means social change. Upheld as art and considered an elevated form of language, poetry comes under suspicion when its language is not an end in itself. Poet June Jordan characterizes the literary activist poets and the resistance they have met. She begins with Whitman:

> There is Whitman and all of the poets whose lives have been baptized by witness to blood, by witness to cataclysmic, political confrontations from the Civil War through the Civil Rights Era, through the Women's Movement, and on and on through the conflicts between the hungry and the well-fed, the wasteful, the bullies.
>
> In the poetry of the New World, you meet with a reverence for the material world that begins with a reverence for human life. There is an intellectual trust in sensuality as a means of knowledge, an easily deciphered system of reference, aspirations to a believable, collective voice and, consequently, emphatic preference for broadly accessible, spoken language. Deliberately balancing perception with vision, it seeks to match moral exhortation with sensory report.
>
> All of the traceable descendants of Whitman have met with an establishment, academic reception disgracefully identical; except for the New World poets who live and write beyond the boundaries of the USA, the offspring of this one white father encounter everlasting marketplace disparagement as crude or optional or simplistic.[7]

For half my life, I have worked with students who have been taught that poetry "should" be obscure and hard to understand. If it is accessible, they at first question whether it is poetry at all.

In school, all too often, they have been denied their own heritage, those New World poets who speak in an "easily deciphered system of reference" and employ a "broadly accessible, spoken language." When they discover such poets exist, they are surprised, amazed, relieved and delighted. Poetry, too, is something they need not feel shut out of. I am reminded of Emily Dickinson's lines: "Why—do they shut Me out of Heaven? / Did I sing—too loud?"[8]

That some might want people to feel shut out of poetry gives us pause. The now infamous moment when then First Lady Laura Bush canceled a symposium, "Poetry and the American Voice," to be held at the White House in February 2003, fearing poets would speak against military action in Iraq, reminds us of the large strain in the United States that would keep its poetry separate from real world events. As the formal statement from the White House read, "While Mrs. Bush understands the rights of all Americans to express their political views, this event was designed to celebrate poetry."[9]

This desire to keep poetry out of the public realm has a long and complicated history in the United States. Were we to consider the eighteenth century alone, for example, we would not be able to separate the two. But the shift into the nineteenth century with its increasing industrialization and emphasis on the United States as the nation of business surfaced the long process of commodifying poetry. Was poetry necessity or was it luxury? How was it valued and by whom? By the mid-twentieth century, perceptions of poetry in the United States were marked by ambivalence, distrust or even disdain. To explain these attitudes might well take several lifetimes. It certainly has been explored by many—some of whom I will bring into conversation for our consideration—though there are many more voices in this discussion.[10]

In the 1840s, Ralph Waldo Emerson noted the ambivalence framed into the rising definition of what it meant to be "American": "In our political parties, compute the power of badges and emblems. . . . In the political processions, Lowell goes in a loom, and Lynn in a shoe, and Salem in a ship. . . . The people fancy they hate poetry, and they are all poets and mystics!"[11] Equating the poetic principle with "the universality of the symbolic language," he notes how every group participates in poetry at the most fundamental level. Humans represent themselves through symbols. We turn poet, or at least toward poetry, with every image we use. Nonetheless, that poetic nature is kept at arm's length. "The people fancy they hate poetry." Already in 1844, contradictory elements within the culture play tug of war with poetry.

A century later, poet and essayist Muriel Rukeyser addressed the "fear of" and "resistance to" poetry in her still undervalued 1949 work *The Life of Poetry*.[12] Writing in the aftermath of World War II and a suddenly nuclear weapons-infused world, she took on the undercurrents roiling in the postwar world. Beneath the societal proclamations that normalcy had returned, insecurity festered. Rukeyser described this period in the United States as a "time of the crises of the spirit."[13] A growing number of people felt threatened by work that was "closest to imagination," and she cited that fear as "evidence of what [in the society] has broken down."[14] Noting an overarching and alarming desire for uniformity, she writes,

> We suffer from that background, with its hunger for uniformity, the shared norm of ambition and habit and living standard. The repressive codes are everywhere. Our movies are censored before they are plotted; our radio comedy is forbidden its list of themes. . . .
>
> Our education is one of specialization. We become experts in some narrow "field." That expertness allows us to deal with the limited problems presented to us; it allows us to face emotional reality, symbolic reality, very little.[15]

With imagination perceived as dangerous and individuals groomed for uniformity and limitation, it is little wonder that poetry goes missing. The people in Emerson's day who still enacted poetry in their daily choices seem entirely absent from the adults Rukeyser describes. Here are people who say they don't understand poetry, are bored by it, don't have time for it, find it "intellectual, confused, unmusical," "willfully obscure," "effeminate."[16] This is more than mild distaste or simple indifference. Something greater is at work, which Rukeyser characterizes as fear.

Her descriptions of the poetry resister clarify who could be found in this group. Given her day and age, someone home from the war and a "first-rate scientist"[17] more likely than not was white and male. It is curious to link "fear" to a group that nominally had the least to fear. Consider the numerous cross burnings on African-American citizens' property. Or how many people couldn't vote. Or if they could, voted as their husbands or fathers instructed. In Rukeyser's writing, fear assumed a markedly different character, but one whose ramifications were felt by all members of the society. She identifies a "psychic problem" plaguing those in power that in turn invariably shaped the conditions in which other members of the society lived. She comments,

> I have found in working with people and with poems, that this fear presents the symptoms of a psychic problem. A poem does invite, it does require. What does it invite? A poem invites you to feel. More than that: it invites you to respond. And better than that: a poem invites a total response.
>
> This response is total, but it is reached through the emotions. A fine poem will seize your imagination intellectually—that is, when you reach it, you will reach it

intellectually too—but the way is through emotion, through what we call feeling.[18]

Her analysis strikes at peculiar, if not unfamiliar, aspects of American mainstream culture. Individualism has never responded kindly when requirements are seemingly "imposed" on the individual. What right has a poem to "require" anything of its reader? And that such requirement functions through emotion is another sticking point for dominant culture. The definition of the American as the practical go-getter keen on efficiency holds little room for "feeling" as its primary source. Amplify that through the long-standing American cultural gendering of emotion as "feminine" or, to use a more revealing word, "effeminate." Who would seek out an association with poetry given those terms? Let alone give a "total response" reached through the emotions? Better to avoid poetry's "requirements," even if they were disguised as invitations.

Pausing for the moment, who has responded to a poem's invitation? Where have we seen such "total response," or perhaps given it? What other traditions do we draw upon, or know intimately, that make such a response not only imaginable but also practical and practicable?

"With this poem as starting point": The reader's role in Ikeda's poetry

In his poems, Ikeda reminds us how large the act of responsive reading is. It comprises many variations, and we daily play across the range. Some focus on words; others on gestures. Some depend more on ears; others on eyes. Different aspects of the mind come into play, and one leads into another. Nor are we alone in this activity. Even when we are at our most solitary, there is always another voice speaking, and we may well be reading in concert with others. In Ikeda's model of reading, the reader is always responding.

One of Ikeda's most striking examples comes from a poem in

which reading is not directly described. In his poem honoring Nataliya Sats, founder of the first children's theater in Moscow, there are no scenes of actors reading lines. The rehearsals themselves are not described. He focuses instead on the context from which such reading emerges. He writes,

> Art is the power to live.
> Like the pulse of spring
> reviving nature,
> the irrepressible energy
> of life itself, breaking through
> suffering and pain,
> to arrive finally at joy.
>
> Art is the power to love.
> A symphony of fraternity
> that continually discovers
> the brilliant jewel
> existing in the heart
> of each and all.
>
> Art is the power
> to believe in each other.
> A multihued bridge
> linking all people,
> founded solidly
> on the universally human
> beyond all individual or national
> differences.
>
> *("Mother of art, the sunlight of happiness," p. 185)*

Art is rendered active: not noun but verb, not an object of study but an always-creating force. It is "an irrepressible energy"; it "continually discovers," and when described as an object, it remains active: the "multihued bridge / linking all people." The repetition that opens each stanza evokes dynamic stability in a world of "irrepressible energy." Each stanza describes transformation. Being, in Ikeda's world of art, means becoming.

What kind of reading leads to this art? If transformation is central, then flexibility of mind is essential. The reader's mind never stays fixed on one point. Reading requires a perpetual enlarging of the mind, grounded in ongoing self-inquiry and self-criticism. There is no rest for the reader, no passivity. In one of his short poems, he outlines the dynamic:

> I read books
>   and I write.
> I happily engage
>   in discussion and debate.
> I choose not to reject
>   even the harshest criticism.
> I want to maintain
>   a spirit of passionate seeking,
>   the ability to respect those
>   who forthrightly point out
>   my failings.
> ("*To my young friends,*" p. 37)

Guided by that principle of "passionate seeking," the "I" of this poem incorporates "even the harshest criticism." The individual chooses "not to reject" such criticism. The easier alternative would be to reject it out of hand, turn defensive and defiant and blame the harshness rather than inquiring into the criticism. Ikeda's emphasis remains on self-examining individual agency. Passive voice does not enter the poem. The reader is invited to speak with the poem's "I." She/he too can "read," "write," "engage," "choose," "maintain."

In Ikeda's world, reading is fundamentally relational. The word

"I"—what might be thought of as a separating voice—is most often a mode of connection, inviting the reader to participate in a shared individual voice. When together we say "I," we most firmly build that "multihued bridge." While "we" might seem the more operative moniker, reality suggests something different. In "we," we can hide. "I" keeps us firmly connected to an important and inescapable sense of agency.

Ikeda's active reader is no fiction but a person readily found within the Soka Gakkai community. Meeting with Ikeda's readers in Japan, I have listened to their descriptions of reading practices and seen the commonplace books that serve as their foundation. I have been in discussion groups where a poem was read as a challenge to action, and each reader discussed the action drawn from a particular section of the poem. I have seen how poems form part of individuals' daily lives and understood how no criteria of length defines a poem. A poem may be as short as a handful of words or pages on end. Neither does a poem need to be confined to a page. In many cases, poetry is born in an eminently aural occasion and continues to resound for the mind's ear long after the actual words have been spoken. With every conversation, the reader's agency comes more clearly into focus.

Since you, my reader, did not happen to be in the room during these discussions, I give you another companion for our shared thought: Louise Rosenblatt, teacher and literary critic, who pioneered the field of reader response criticism.[19] In the 1930s, she called for a complex methodology for literary interpretation that paid close and critical attention to readers themselves. In *Literature as Exploration* (1938), she argued the importance of a multidisciplinary approach. She remarks: "To view literature in its living context is to reject any limiting approach, social or aesthetic. Although the social and aesthetic elements in literature may be theoretically *distinguishable*, they are actually *inseparable*."[20] Her emphasis was always on the actual: what happens when a person reads. Twenty-five years later in "The Poem as Event" (1964), she writes, "A poem, then, must be thought of as an event in time. It is not an object or an ideal entity. It is an occurrence, a coming together, a compenetration, of a reader and a text. The reader brings to the text his past experience; the encounter gives rise to a new experience, a poem."[21] In an expanded version of this essay published in *The Reader, the Text, the Poem*, Rosenblatt continues to develop the difference between text on the page and poem as event. She writes, "A poem should not be thought of as an object, an entity, but rather as an active process lived through during the relationship between a reader and a text." The poem, she asserts, does not exist "apart from author or reader."[22] She likens the situation to music, where the musical notation on the page is not by itself music but a means by which music becomes possible.[23]

Here was very much what I had experienced in conversations with the women of the Soka Gakkai, whether with members of the Women's Peace Committee or students at Soka Women's College. Poetry was not something an individual "received," or in the more colloquial lingo of my students "got," but something actively participated in. Rosenblatt emphasized the role and full extent of the reader's experience. In contrast to New Criticism, which considered actual readers' experiences to be intrusions into interpretation, Rosenblatt's reader-response criticism focused on the active work of the reader. That this was work, she made clear. Individuals did not simply make poems mean what they wanted. They had to be scrupulously careful about their own imposition upon a poem. While they could draw on personal experience (and, as she argued, it was almost impossible for people to so distance themselves as to not draw upon their own experiences), they could not substitute experience for the poem. Readers' experiences informed their reading; they also, as Rosenblatt argued, allowed the reader to enter the poem through feeling rather than treating the poem as something from which meaning could be obtained as so many facts from an informative article.

Rosenblatt draws the distinction between two types of reading, calling the latter "efferent" from the Latin root "to bear" or "to carry." In an efferent reading, the reader concentrates on factual summary and information extracted from the text. With the former, what she termed "aesthetic" reading, the emphasis is on immediacy and process. Rosenblatt writes, "The reader must have the experience, must 'live through' what is being created during the reading."[24] Here is where Ikeda's Japanese readers do most of their work, although the efferent reading seemingly appears when the words are carried into action. However, a striking difference separates the reading I have observed from the efferent Rosenblatt describes. For Ikeda's Japanese readers, the reference point of personal experience, how the poem felt in the moment of reading and studying, is not replaced by the idea carried away from the poem. The two remain intertwined.

On a bright October day in 2012, I returned for my second visit to the Soka International Women's Center to meet with women from both the Women's Peace Committee and the Young Women's Conference for Peace and Culture. Part of the Soka Gakkai International, the largest lay Buddhist organization in the world, these women share the organization-wide commitment to ongoing dialogue as the foundation for human understanding. Originating in the early twentieth century, the Soka Gakkai arose from Tsunesaburo Makiguchi's revolutionary educational reforms. Makiguchi strongly opposed Japan's increasingly militarized education with its dehumanizing consequences for the individual. He developed an educational system that focused on developing the distinct and creative potential within each student. Jailed by the Japanese government in 1943 along with one of his colleagues, Josei Toda, Makiguchi died in prison before World War II ended.

Upon his release from prison in 1945, Toda continued Makiguchi's work, focusing on the threat posed to each person's humanity by a world where nuclear weapons determined the so-called balance of power. In 1957, he issued a landmark declaration in Yokohama calling for the abolition of all nuclear armaments. Upon Toda's death, Daisaku Ikeda took up where Toda left off, continuing the ongoing work toward a nuclear-weapons-free world as well as foregrounding the importance of education, especially education of the "poetic heart."

Both the educative and the poetic were at the forefront of the conversations I shared with women members of the Soka Gakkai during my visit to Japan in 2012. The setting was itself symbolic. The Soka International Women's Center is designed as a place where women can speak freely among themselves and pursue intellectual inquiry and societal work on their own terms. The Center hosts public lectures, exhibitions, as well as smaller meetings, along with the everyday work of the various women's division offices. The Center often features lectures and seminars on peace as well as providing a welcoming home within which to discuss the ongoing work of the Women's Peace Committee and the Young Women's Conference for Peace and Culture. That work is longstanding and monumental.

Consider the Women's Peace Committee's decade-long work (1981–91) during which they engaged in an extensive gathering of oral and written history, compiling twenty volumes of war testimonials from women who had lived through World War II in Japan. Knowing that women's experiences of war often go unrecorded, women of the Peace Committee met with hundreds of women who survived the war, including those who had been in Hiroshima and Nagasaki during the atomic bombings. They listened to their stories, mourned with the women and supported them in the difficult work of sharing the horror of the violence they had experienced.

In addition to the published volumes, the Women's Peace Committee produced a DVD (2006) that includes the war experiences of thirty-one women who survived the nuclear weapons' devastation of Hiroshima and Nagasaki. The committee has also created large-scale exhibitions focusing on cultures of peace.

The Young Women's Conference for Peace and Culture has taken on the ongoing need for peace education among youth, both in fact-finding and in curriculum development that effectively reaches people of their generation. In each project, these women model an inclusive dialogue that welcomes every voice and calls each participant to large-minded, clear-hearted listening.

During my 2012 visit to the Center, thirty of us met around tables—a classroom setting—as they had promised to be "my students" for the day. In truth, we were students and teachers to one another and took turns leading the discussion. In a tradition after my own heart, we got down to the work of sharing thought through the essential act of sharing food—green tea and traditional sweets that were as beautiful to the eye as to the taste. There were, of course, cranes folded from golden paper, three of which now sit on one of my bookshelves. Some might think of these as pleasantries—and pleasant it certainly was to sip the tea, a taste I can never duplicate in Hamilton, New York—but it was by no means the trivial event such a word "pleasantry" has come to mean. We were tuning our minds, attending to one another, beginning to forge a place and pace for conversation—a rhythm for sharing. As Rosenblatt might remind us, poems differ depending upon where, when and with whom they are read. It behooves us to pay attention to the circumstances of our reading, lest we miss the poem itself.

For discussion, the women had chosen "August 15—The dawn of a new day" (pp. 340–52). As with nearly all of Ikeda's long poems, this was first published in the *Seikyo Shimbun*, a Japanese daily newspaper (circulation of 5.5 million) published by the Soka Gakkai with wide-ranging coverage from national and international news to developments in science and health to features on

Soka Gakkai events and members. This poem first appeared in print on August 15, 2001, fifty-six years to the day of Japan's surrender in World War II. A scathing critique of war, Ikeda's poem focuses on the experiences apart from the so-called battlefield. In a series of vignettes, he shows older couples attempting to find shelter during air raids, and his own brothers turned into pawns for the war. The day of surrender is a day of relief as his parents imagine the safe return of their sons and his mother prepares dinner. He singles out her delight over light. No longer need they hide in the commanded darkness of wartime.

Each of the six women from the respective peace committees chose to focus on a different section of the poem. Akemi Tsukiji began, reading aloud the third and fourth stanzas for their evocation of the "hardship and suffering [that] were forced on ordinary citizens."

> A day of penitence
> recalling the senseless
> battlefield deaths
> of so many millions
> of loved ones.
>
> A day of eternal parting
> from sweethearts and lovers.
> A day of tears
> for mothers who would
> never again see their dear children.
> A day of hopeless heartbreak,
> learning that young sons
> —the future hope of their families
> and society as a whole—
> were never to return.
> A day of anguished grief

as fathers, too, shed bitter tears . . .
The fifteenth of August—
Ah, August 15!

Emphasizing the "strong antiwar sentiment" of the poem, she sounded the note that would resound through the rest of the discussion. "With this poem as a starting point": the poem was the point of departure, but never in the sense of leaving the poem behind. Each woman singled out a different section and then thought through the words to the action they undertook. In almost every case, Ikeda's words opened a way for other voices to be heard. In the poem's balance between his own personal experience and the more generalized evocations of all who experienced the war, space opened for others' stories to be told.

Picking up the discussion where Ms. Tsukiji left off, Michiko Shiotsu connected three sections from the poem that highlight the ordinary person's experience of war.

Ah, August 15, 1945!
That day the summer sky
was bright and brilliant.

At noon there was
a radio broadcast announcing
Japan's defeat.
Invincible Japan,
so certain of victory,
had been thoroughly beaten.
Many wept,
but far more, no doubt,
felt relief
deep in their hearts.

. . . .

On that day of August 15,
my father, face flushed with emotion,
murmured to himself,
"My sons will now return. . . ."

. . . .

My diminutive mother
prepared dinner,
excited as a young girl:
"How bright it is!
Now we can keep the lights on!
How lovely and bright!"

. . . .

How good, they thought,
how good that the war
is over at last.

Noting that every war survivor greeted the war's end with relief, Ms. Shiotsu also commented that many of the women initially "had no wish to ever talk about their war experiences. . . . There were things they had never even shared with their families." These women, however, resolved to retell the trauma rather than silence it. She highlighted each woman's sense of urgency. Knowing the persistence of war's suffering in the contemporary world, they told the actual stories of war rather than the glorified versions. It was their part in "creating a peaceful world."

Those fuller stories poured forth in the women's subsequent comments. Nanae Kimura highlighted the stanzas where Ikeda mulls over the aching fact that human beings who normally oppose war can in fact be turned into human beings who actively support it:

> None of us had wanted
> this war.
> We had never
> accepted or supported it.
>
> Yet over time
> almost without noticing,
> we were all influenced,
> maneuvered and brainwashed
> to extol the glories of war.
>
> The human heart holds
> terrible possibilities.
> More terrible still
> are those who use their power
> to mold and manipulate
> people's minds.

Addressing the question that haunts us all, Ms. Kimura first spoke about her own inquiry into that potent contradiction in human behavior. Why do those with the greatest interest in sustaining life turn to support its destruction? She talked about the power of survivors' testimonies—whether the woman who had fallen prey to "militaristic education" so that she valued her son's war death more highly than his life or the nurse who saw how the words that were "supposed" to be on a dying soldier's lips were rarely delivered. More often than not, "Mother" replaced "Long live the Emperor."

For every person in the discussion, the question was not "what does this mean" but "what shall we, or what shall I, do?" The poet's words returned to the reader herself. They became the germinating seeds for action. Whether Ms. Kimura speaking about the importance of women's resistance to all attempts at mental manipulation or Mutsuko Kinoshita from the Young Women's Conference for Peace and Culture discussing peace work among Japanese youth, verbal agency was central. The word's transformative power was key. Poetic words encouraged others, whether that encouragement took the form of silenced stories finally shared or of educative programs undertaken.

During the conversation, it became clear that this poem was an old friend for many of the women. Not only did their remarks suggest multiple readings across the years since it was first published, but their response to my inquiry about when and how they first encountered the poem led to a fascinating conversation about reading practices themselves. As noted, the poem was first published on August 15, 2001, in the *Seikyo Shimbun*. Given the practice of reading aloud with one another, it would not have been surprising for even the youngest in the room to have heard the poem at that time, even if they were then only eight or nine years old.

What happened next is a practice that crosses many places and times. Readers cut the poems from the newspaper and assemble them within the covers of their own selected notebooks, essentially creating their own poetry volumes. In the United States, I have followed this practice from the eighteenth-century commonplace books of Milcah Martha Moore to a nature-focused collection kept in camp by two women who built a cabin in the Adirondacks in the 1920s to my own grandmother's "repurposing" of an algebra textbook into a selection of popular poetry. In conversations in Japan, I learned that the practice is almost exclusively focused among the women's division members. There was laughter about how young women use smaller notebooks because their eyesight is better, but throughout, the conversation focused on the reader's role. As one woman said, "Each person has her own way of collecting these clippings." I include a piece of the transcript from the conversation, conducted through an interpreter, to give a sense of the liveliness involved in the discussion prompted by my question about how they read Ikeda's poetry:

WOMAN 1: At first, we see it in the *Seikyo Shimbun*. Later, it becomes published in book form so we can read it again in the book. The first encounter, though, is always in the newspaper.

WOMAN 2: Newspapers tend to get lost, but of course, when poems are compiled into a book, we can read them repeatedly.

WOMAN 3: We women's division members, especially, always cut out those pages. [Laughter]

SARAH WIDER: I was wondering about that. I thought you probably did, but I wanted to know for sure.

WOMAN 4: So we cut them out and paste them in notebooks, which we carry around with us all the time.

WOMAN 5: *The New Human Revolution*, which is a serialized novel, is published in the newspaper every day. So we hold onto the newspaper clippings. When it becomes published as a book, we decide that our "mission" of collecting clippings is over for the time being. [Laughter] Every day there is a new illustration but the book doesn't include them all, so some people like to keep the newspaper clippings just for the illustrations.

WOMAN 6: There are people who pride themselves on having kept newspaper clippings of the entire serialized novel.

WOMAN 7: Most newspapers are meant to be read and thrown away. But for us, the *Seikyo Shimbun* is like a letter from President Ikeda, so we treasure the newspaper clippings.

WOMAN 8: Once President Ikeda's poems appear in a book we'll read them, and each time we read them we are encouraged by a different aspect. . . . So it is very important that they become published in a book. In various situations, we will open a page and what we read will elicit a different response. President Ikeda's words continue to touch us in a way unique to our present circumstance. That is why we treasure the publications.

While the commonplace books become a source of friendly rivalry, they also highlight differences between means of publication. The newspaper offers something the later publication can never duplicate. The initial occasion of one's reading; the events attached to that time, the responses, the particulars of individual experience wrapped up in that moment of reading: the newspaper clipping as well as the comments written in the notebook speak directly of and to that time. In the case of *The New Human Revolution*, this also includes the novel's illustrations. However, keeping those associations so clearly allied may well interfere with future readings. The book publication offers readers a fresh encounter for their "current situation." It allows the poem to speak more readily in a "different way." Not to mention that those who may have missed the original publication would then have access to the poems through the book's publication.

Students in a special seminar at Soka Women's College coordinated by Professor Toshiko Nagashima also focused on how poems provoke action. In keeping with the poem under discussion ("May the fragrant laurels of happiness adorn your life"), they emphasized the reader and her day-to-day choices. Those choices, however, evoked a world far larger than a single self. Each comment predicated the constructive power of poetic language. For example, one young woman described the multiple speakers a certain metaphor brought to mind. Quoting the lines "Just as the lamp you light for another / will illuminate your own way,"[25] she talked about her mother as a prominent source for the power of these words. During a difficult time of near bullying in middle school, her mother's reflections on these words enabled her to see beyond the daily darkness she experienced. Returning to Ikeda's words, she framed them as a shared discourse in work that matters: "President Ikeda talks to us a great deal about this kind of chain reaction of care and concern for other people; this is the ultimate foundation for world peace."

Students noted the value of reading poetry together. For those who had attended Soka schools, the approach was familiar. For others, it was new. All agreed on its value:

STUDENT 1: His poetry was always part of our educational experience. My friends and I would read and study the poetry together in class and share our opinions and views. For me, this was always very helpful, because there were aspects of the poetry that friends would point out that had not even occurred to me. So through them, I would realize the deeper meaning of the poem—what Ikeda Sensei had in mind when he created it. So for me, reading and discussing his poetry together has been the best way to study and gain a deeper understanding of Ikeda Sensei and his poetic spirit.

STUDENT 2: For me, this was invaluable because it was really a chance to get to know my friends better, because when they spoke about the poetry they interpreted it in terms of their personal experience—from their heart. In this way, I felt I got to know their true thoughts and feelings.

The first student focused on the poetry itself. When multiple readers come together in shared discussion, they see what would otherwise go unnoticed. The collective approach extends individual readers beyond their own limited perspectives and thus works as a tool for building a more fully dimensioned understanding. The second student focused on the readers and the friendships made possible or strengthened by their shared reading. As she said, their willingness to draw upon personal experience created an environment in which friendships flourished.

Whether the focus was the text or the reader, the collaborative elements of reading stood out both here and in my conversations with other women's division members. In addition to the discussion of "August 15" with the Women's Peace Committee and the Young Women's Conference for Peace and Culture, I also spoke with women who casually referred to study sessions focusing on Ikeda's words, whether poetry or prose. This shared quality of reading reflects another aspect of the poetry's reception. While many initially read Ikeda's poetry in the *Seikyo Shimbun*, others hear it on its first public delivery. While that audience is, by definition, "of the occasion," there are also numerous subsequent situations where Ikeda's poetry is shared as song.[26]

"A TORRENT OF LANGUAGE": COMPOSING THE POEMS

To begin to understand the fullness of Ikeda's poetry requires the ear as much as the eye. It also asks us to detach ourselves from images of the solitary poet in a garret. Nowhere can this more readily be seen than in Ikeda's composition process. With the exception of the early poems, his poetry is composed, not written. Creating the poem is an event shared with others and requires their active listening.

Shigeo Hasegawa, Yumiko Kasanuki and Kayo Maeta are three

people who, since their youth, have been trained by and have worked closely with Ikeda.[27] They recalled situations of feverish writing, each person trying to record the words as quickly as Ikeda spoke them. They characterized Ikeda's great facility with language in terms of a swift flow: "a pouring out," "a torrent of language," "speaking as if water were flowing from a stream." Each called attention to his staggering ability to keep track of what he had said despite being interrupted during the process of composition.

Describing the composition of "Youth, scale the mountain of kosen-rufu of the twenty-first century" (pp. 62–76), Ms. Kasanuki noted how Ikeda left to meet with a pioneer Soka Gakkai member after the first forty minutes of working on the poem—forty minutes, it is worth observing, in which he spoke without pause. He asked them to create a clean copy while he was gone. He had no notes with him. During the time he was at the member's house, he contacted them and asked that they make a particular addition, citing the exact place where the words should be added. Ms. Kasanuki remarked on the amazement she and her fellow workers shared, wondering how it was possible to keep the poem so clearly in his mind with no visual prompts. She pointed out the great length of the poem—twelve pages. It is not a length most carry readily in their mind.

Ms. Maeta described a similar occasion in which the composition process was interrupted, only to be resumed as if there had been no pause. She recalled an occasion in June 1981 during Ikeda's visit to France. As they were boarding the train to leave Paris for Sceaux, he exclaimed, "Let's compose a poem now." He began speaking the minute they boarded the train and continued even while they were transferring. At that point some French Soka Gakkai members came up to Ikeda for a moment's conversation. The composition process stopped, only to resume as if it had never been interrupted.

Ms. Maeta commented: "After he had finished speaking with

the members, he asked me, 'Where did we leave off?' So he continued reciting his poem from where he had been interrupted. From my illegible jottings, I made a clean version. He made revisions from that. By the time we arrived at the community center, the poem was ready, the poem was complete." Well, not entirely. As she concluded the story, she commented on the difficult work facing the translator who then had to translate the Japanese into a French that the evening's audience would admire.

Mr. Hasegawa also noted a close connection between travel and Ikeda's poems. In his estimation, of the poems he has been involved in, "about 90 percent of his poems have been written in the car." The pace is frenetic, with each person writing as quickly as he or she can. He described the scene: "President Ikeda's wife often sits next to him in the back seat. She is very fast at taking notes. She can tell that I'm not keeping up with the pace. When we get out of the car, she will quickly pass me her notes and say, 'Here, I hope this helps you.' And there it is. So when we make a clean copy, putting them together, we give that to President Ikeda and he will approve it, maybe making some comments and changes."

All the same, it is difficult to channel the whole torrent. Mr. Hasegawa commented on his frustration and sense of responsibility: "I really feel terrible about it. . . . We may have overlooked or missed writing down something really important." Where they have lost words, the transcribers leave open space. Ikeda then may re-create the passage with new phrases, new resonances celebrating the always ongoing poetic process of making meaning.

Attention to others surfaces in all elements of the poetic process. In Ms. Kasanuki's recounting of "Youth, scale the mountain," she drew attention to the fact that the member Ikeda visited during the composition of the poem was the mother of one of the individuals who was working on the transcription. The mother's description of her son figured into the poem. It is this description that Ikeda called into the group during his time away. When the poem was finished, Ikeda asked the son to read the new poem for the youth meeting then under way.[28]

Given these descriptions, it would seem that Ikeda lives in a world of creative fluency. In contrast to an image of words as containers of meaning, more appropriate is the torrent of language that never runs dry. Citing a comment from Mrs. Ikeda, Ms. Kasanuki reflected on the correspondent flow between creative energy of language and creative flux of the universe. She commented, "Mrs. Ikeda once said: 'In Japanese we write poems vertically, not horizontally, like English. However, my husband does not write vertically with breaks between every line but in a circular motion without pause. Words continue to pour forth as if it were the flow of the universe.'"

Encountering Ikeda's poetry in its composition, both Ms. Kasanuki and Mrs. Ikeda drew attention to the multiple dimensions the poetry involves. Figured spatially, their descriptions take us off the page (as well as reminding English readers that the horizontal spacing of words to which we are accustomed is only the convention of one language system). In reading Ikeda's poetry, it is wise to remember that the poem, most likely, was composed as part of an aural process and may well have first been designed for an aural occasion. Such is the "reading" practice powerfully described by those in Ishinomaki after the devastating tsunami of March 11, 2011. When Ikeda's words of encouragement in the *Seikyo Shimbun* arrived on March 13, there was only a single copy. The message was read aloud to those taking refuge in a Soka Gakkai facility that was opened to the public as an emergency shelter after the tsunami struck Ishinomaki. How the words were initially written on the page would have been invisible to all but the reader. In conversations with those present, their reports are much more akin to Ms. Kasanuki's description of "the flow of the universe." In this case, the words provided the restorative rhythm after the chaos of the tsunami.

"An unshakable state of life": Poetry and encouragement

Ikeda's words in and for that moment call attention to his vital aesthetic. A spirit of encouragement is integral to the poetry and inseparable from it. Directly linking the two, Mr. Hasegawa remarks: "This practice of encouragement, for him, is everything. When he composes poems—whether long or short—his single-minded determination is, 'I'm going to enable this person to become happy without fail. I have to do something for this person.' The momentary crystallization of that spirit, that heart, becomes the poem—it turns into language immediately."

In many ways, this dynamic between encouragement and poetry can be traced to the educative element within the Soka Gakkai. The focus rests on creating value rather than analyzing, consuming or protecting it. The dynamic is thus generative and collaborative. The outlook is expansive, emphasizing what can be nurtured and sustained. Within the Buddhist understanding, this also integrally involves perceiving the profound interconnectedness that underlies all existence. At the same time, respect for complex interdependence requires constant courage and, indeed, an ongoing state of encouragement. To work actively and consistently for peace in a violence-laden world is far more difficult than even the greatest cynic could contend. It demands deliberate and thought-full choices made in each moment. There can be no lapse of attentiveness. Human minds are rarely attuned to such rigor. It is all too common to lose heart.

In the context of the disheartened and discouraged, it is worth looking at Ikeda's focus on those within marginalized groups. Who lacks access to full participation, not only in their societies but in their very humanity? Nowhere is encouragement more prevalent than within Ikeda's poetry written for and about women and for and about youth. Now, before the cry of "women and children first" drowns out the discussion, consider the absence of real agency for most young people or the historic and continued oppression women face across place and time. Ikeda describes this reality for women in his poem "Mother" (pp. 51–59), written in 1971:

> The history of women
> has been darkened
> by torment,
> extinguished smiles,
> and pained, despairing tears.
> The time has now come
> to relegate that history
> to an ancient, fossil past.

Forty years after this poem was composed, some would maintain that Ikeda's call has been answered and that "history" has been "relegated" to "an ancient, fossil past." And it is true that *some* women and *some* young people have been brought into existing power structures. But the inherent problem remains unsolved. Those very structures exist by acts of exclusion. A few from the marginalized groups may be admitted, but it is only a few. As Adrienne Rich says so well,

> Power withheld from the vast majority of women [or of any historically underrepresented group of people] is offered to a few, so that it appears that any truly qualified woman can gain access to leadership, recognition, and reward. . . . The token woman is encouraged to see herself as different from most other women, as exceptionally talented and deserving, and to separate herself from the wider female condition.[29]

The cost of access may well be yourself. Without substantive change to a system founded upon your exclusion, you may well find yourself becoming what you are not: an honorary man, an honorary white person, an honorary adult. In the centers of power, gone are the voices that actually speak the multifold experiences of working women and marginalized youth. Even those designations say so little and threaten to silence so much. To that end, Ikeda seeks to create what he would call a constant symphony of language in which all people can play their part, sometimes solo, more often in the section from within which their story can best sing. Those officially or subtly silenced have every need of strongly felt courage. Taking English at its word, "encouragement" describes a process of sharing, giving strength or heart (cour) to another. Ikeda defines this as the poet's main work (and indeed humanity's fundamental way of being in this world).

His poem for the young women's division "Fragrant laurels of happiness" gives a tour de force of his poetic strategies of encouragement. The poem opens with praise for the sun. Introduced, as if on its own terms, it is singled out for its revelatory power as well as its undeterred and undeterrable illumination:

> How beautiful is the sun,
> its limitless, multihued lights revealing
> the inherent dignity of humankind!
> This undeniable force,
> this unfaltering existence dedicated
> to fulfilling its vow,
> to illuminating all things for all time!

The next stanza turns on a series of declarative statements. As if fulfilling the power evoked in the opening lines, we see the kind of world constituted by such power. The power that "illuminat[es] all things for all time" makes possible a world in which "there is no discrimination" and "the same rights are shared by all." The stanza reads with chant-like force with its threefold repetition of "In the presence of the sun."

> In the presence of the sun
> there is no darkness.
> In the presence of the sun
> there is no discrimination.
> In the presence of the sun
> the same rights are shared by all
> and a world of peace shines brightly.

In these opening stanzas, the speaking voice is strong and affirming but not assigned to a single person. It may be a choral voice or an individual, a personal voice or one larger than any single human being. In the third stanza, we make our first acquaintance with the first person.

> Today once more
> I will walk my chosen path
> pursue my chosen work
> bring my history to new luster.
> Undeterred by deceitful rains,
> I will walk a path of bright smiles
> true to myself, as only I can,
> undefeated by anything!
> For I understand this path
> to be my treasured way.

Here is an "I" that speaks with kindred affirmation. The verbs are punctuated by the determined "will": "I will walk my chosen path / pursue my chosen work." The adjectives are similarly strong: "undeterred," "undefeated." The speaker vows to remain "true to myself," regardless of the "heartless criticism" that comes as the ready response to those who live with such conviction.

The unidentified speaker readily gives readers the opportunity to take this "I" as their own. While one might assume this is Ikeda's voice, the next stanzas with their emphasis on being young and in that moment building the very "foundations / of a lifetime," suggest that the "I" belongs to someone in their first decades:

> Youth—
> this time in life that comes but once,
> dignified and precious
> like a glittering gem.
> I will live vivaciously, with all my might.
> Because to do so is to lay the foundations
> of a lifetime,
> and from here is born a new happiness
> arising from the very core of my being.

Gradually, another speaker enters the poem. It is not easy to say where. Even when the telltale "you" appears and one looks back at the previous stanza, it is not clear exactly where this voice enters.

> Of course there will be bad times
> along with the good.
> But I will never hurl insults at life.
>
> The growing vital force that is youth—
> in each joyous stride
> there is so much to read and learn
> so much wisdom to seek.
>
> Whatever the blizzards of this life
> you can emerge triumphant
> by the strengths residing
> within your heart.

In the first stanza of this passage, the informal and conversational nature of the language suggests that the young woman is still speaking. The beginning of the next stanza may well raise a question with its shift of tone at the beginning, but then it returns to the more informal and conversational. Only with the "you" are we reminded that another voice is present. Within the poem as a whole, this gives no jolt. The opening stanzas have already alerted us to multivocal possibilities with their unspecified speakers.

Taking up this question of the different "I's" with both the Soka Women's College students as well as with other Soka Gakkai members, the conversations turned on how seamlessly that shift occurred from one "I" to another. As speakers of English and also for those unfamiliar with Soka Gakkai reading communities, we may not be as alert to an "I" that is simultaneously yours and mine. In part, this lies within the structure of Japanese with its different forms of "I" and different tones within each form. In part, it also depends, as Rosenblatt would say, upon the experience that readers bring to the poem. Those familiar with Ikeda's life and language bring that knowledge with them. If they are aware of the struggles Ikeda faced during his youth, they may well hear the speaking "I" of those earlier stanzas referring to Ikeda and the reader in an aural palimpsest of past and present.

It also readily allows the reader to stand in the familiar Soka Gakkai relation of mentor and pupil. Given the Soka Gakkai's foundation in educational reform and Ikeda's own lifelong commitment to education, the conversation between "you" and "I" can be framed as a dialogue between teacher and student. In this poem, as in many others, the distinct nature of this relationship is defined by the fact that the teacher does not stand above the pupil but beside him or her. Without this mutuality, a dialogue would be impossible.

Ikeda strengthens the dialogic quality of the poem by allowing other voices to speak. They may be contemporary or from centuries past. These are not simply "cameo" appearances where distinguished figures spout the wisdom most popularly associated with them. In contrast, they speak from dimensions of their lives that most closely address the poem's occasion. In the case of "Fragrant laurels of happiness," the reader hears from the famed violinist Yehudi Menuhin as well as from the nineteenth-century freedom fighter and advocate for Cuba's independence José Martí. Menuhin's words, however, do not speak about music, nor do Martí's speak about liberty. In each case, the speaker enters directly, with words timely to the poem's occasion. The quotation from Menuhin addresses the divinity within all human beings. The words appear in a section that emphasizes humanity's fundamental equality: "No one in this world is better than others. / We are all equally, ordinarily human." Extending the power of this "equal, ordinary humanity," Ikeda focuses the subsequent stanzas on individual choice. Returning to the "I" who is clearly the young woman, the speaker says,

> My joy is not confined
> within a narrow room.
> There is space for all to enter,
> for this friend and that.

Speaking of the "warm camaraderie" of inclusion, Ikeda introduces Martí's words to redefine strength. Strength is not might but the power to be kind. "Kindness," Martí has said, "is the flower of strength." Throughout the rest of the poem, Ikeda continues to develop this image of a strength that flowers in kindness. In the very next stanza, a flower, essentially strength's bloom, is put to the test of "pelting rains." The images recall the opening where the stalwart "I" is "undeterred by deceitful rains." The stanzas call upon the individual to embody that earlier determination to remain "undefeated" whether the challenges come from beyond or within the self. Phrases function as both exhortation and affirmation. He writes, "Be strong! Ever strong!" Such strength requires tough self-inquiry ("reject self-deception") that keeps the individual clear of self-interest ("I will not drown in the / illusory images of renown"). It also presupposes attentiveness beyond the self, to the natural world at all times and in all places, here figured as the two celestial objects that most strikingly greet human vision:

> Make companions
> of the sun and the moon
> as they shine with undying light!

This imagery reminds us that the greatest deception of all is failure to value what is daily with us. Even a person known to history as "extraordinary" returns to the reader as an ordinary individual, no better, no worse.

The rest of the poem celebrates life in its actuality. Speakers shift between two "I's." The first addresses a collective you; the second speaks its own determination. The mentor's guidance shifts into the student's affirmation and acknowledgment of lessons learned:

> Only you know the reality
> of your own life.
> The scorn of others
> based on their personal perception
> is nothing more than that.
> Live true to yourself—
> . . . .
>
> I possess the mirror
> of pristine life
> that reflects with unsparing clarity
> . . . .
>
> I possess the jewel-encrusted
> sword of an idealism that makes

the corrupt and unscrupulous
tremble in shame!

These metaphorical tools make all the more sense with the poem's final major rhetorical device. Menuhin's and Martí's words are incorporated into this poetic dialogue; Joan of Arc's actions enter as the concluding catalyst. Immediately after the imagery of mirror and sword, the addressees in the poem are called "Joan of Arc for the coming era." While this identity seemingly offers an extraordinary role model for the reader, Ikeda reverses the expectation. He writes,

> History recounts
> that Joan of Arc
> was just an ordinary girl.
> But the people of the village
> where she lived described her
> as a young woman of initiative.
>
> She willingly worked,
> she readily spun,
> she gladly pulled the plow . . .
> And when the time came,
> she took the lead
> to fight and rescue
> France from peril!

History's label is far too reductive for experience's reality. Calling Joan "just an ordinary girl," it subordinates the ordinary and remains deaf to the people's voice. The villagers' descriptions of Joan as a "young woman of initiative" offer a different perspective. They illuminate the complexity as well as the powerful familiarity that comprises the ordinary. Sketching her daily actions with the broadest brush, Ikeda creates an interesting triangulation of initiative, flexibility in work and willingness to lead. Joan would do whatever work needed to be done, whether the fields needed plowing or clothing needed to be made. She was active in that work, an initiator who did not simply wait to be told. And in Ikeda's telling, she was a person who took the lead because her daily life had prepared her. To quote from the guidance given earlier in the poem, Joan's early life was spent in "quiet[ly] striving / on the ground of daily living." She was a person who "live[d] out [her] life in its actuality / —in the midst of reality." The reciprocal relation opens. The words that apply to those addressed in the poem apply to Joan herself. Those written about Joan offer a description for others to embody in twenty-first-century form.

Returning to the poem's opening invocation to the sun, Ikeda's use of this imagery reveals an aspect of encouragement many may overlook. While we may think of encouragement as a deeply personal act between two closely related people or between two people imagined to be closely related, Ikeda's use of the sun reminds his reader of its powerfully impersonal nature. The sun erects no boundaries. Its rays include all. It does not depend upon a particular kind of relationship in order to give light, nor does it expect a particular response from what it illumines. It shines all the same. Through this imagery we see a key to Ikedean encouragement: it makes no conditions, nor is it daunted by (apparent) lack of response or even lack of promise. In this, it shows its kinship with another vital element in Ikeda's writings: compassion. Here too the sun's imagery is prominent:

> Real compassion does not depend
> on the other person.
> Just as the sun sheds its light
> equally on all,
> the compassionate person,
> with a broad and open mind,
> an unshakable state of life,

can love, comfort and embrace
any person.
("Youthful country with a shining future," p. 143)

The language is simple and direct. Using a familiar form of comparison, Ikeda gives substance to abstraction. The diffident vagueness of "a broad and open mind" turns into palpable action: light and warmth ("love, comfort and embrace") extend equally to all.

In Ikeda's imagined universe, twin suns illuminate human action. His sun imagery applies both to the young person and to the mother. That both command such power in his poetry may well reflect the fact that each commands so little sustained power in contemporary societies. Actively using language to change perception, he directly challenges readers by bringing them up short against their own unexamined assumptions. Have they bought into existing power structures that cast them in no-win situations of perpetual subordination? We see this even in his use of the word *sun*. Here is something that English does not reveal for its reader. In Japanese, the word for sun is *nichi*, and indeed, the historical Nichiren renamed himself by combining lotus with sun.[30] Thus, the very mention of the sun evokes a primary leader or mentor. Or in this case, perhaps we should say "womentor."

In Ikeda's poetry, mothers enact a sun-like compassion. As might be expected, the force within such compassion is likened to the unrelenting energy reserved for the sun. Clarity defines them. Undaunted by criticism, no doomed circumstance sways them. Ikeda writes,

> Your powers of perception
> are unrivaled by
> any prosecuting attorney.
> *("Salute to mothers," p. 252)*

He terms mothers "unmatched master[s] / of conversation" ("Mother," p. 51) who possess "doctoral degree[s] / in daily living" ("Salute to mothers," p. 250). Through uncompromising observation, the mother develops a distinctive breadth of perspective. Hers is a viewpoint that powerfully comprehends the complexities of the whole. Her wisdom, Ikeda maintains, gives the final lie to the specious logic of "bare-knuckled pride." In "Mother" (pp. 51–59), first published during the Vietnam War, Ikeda calls upon a life philosophy unrestricted by human limitations. He writes,

. . . Mother,
the philosopher, calls out:
People!
Think quietly and deeply.
Behind each of you
is a mother
single-mindedly yearning
for your growth!
The American soldier in Vietnam
has a mother,
fiercely concerned
for her child's life.
The Vietcong soldier
trapped in smoking ruins,
has an agonized mother,
praying for the safety
of her child,
awaiting his return.

The compassionate
love of mothers
knows nothing
of fettering language,

> of the high ice walls
> of nationality,
> of the conflicts and
> struggles of ideology.
> The love of mothers,
> like the narrow path
> between lush green fields,
> is the one emotion
> connecting all people everywhere.

Ikeda casts the mother as the philosopher who commends and indeed commands original thought from her listener. Characterized by quietness and depth, her stance implies a distance from the noise of any established school of thought. It returns all people without exception to their birth, and to the fact that someone cared for them. As we know, human infants fail to thrive without such care. Ikeda defines this care as the mother's "fierce concern" for her own child's life and then expands that concern into the "compassionate / love of mothers" that considers all human beings one's children. When every person is your child and compassion is your guiding principle, no child can be sacrificed in the name of nation or ideology.

In the twentieth and into the twenty-first century, we may well not know what to do with such images of universal mother. Cautioning us against romanticizing the "maternal," biologists remind us that female mammals give birth to and take care of their young according to the needs of the species. Sociologists remind us that any concept of "mother" is a humanly created construct used as a means for social order. Historians remind us that maternal ideals have often included active support of warrior sons. Advocates for women's rights remind us how readily women have been turned into second-class citizens because they were essentialized within a maternal ideal. Even Ikeda acknowledges, in the stanzas previous to the ones quoted, that the "Mother" he describes may well be seen as a "soft and sentimental wish." "They may laugh," he continues,

> and ask how
> such a fragile prayer
> could possibly lead
> the human throng
> out of the dark, dense,
> chaotic woods into which
> we have strayed so deeply . . .

Anticipating the criticism, Ikeda calls attention to the common, societal tendency to dismiss women as "sentimental" or "idealistic" for their critique of existing policy. Their words will be called "a fragile prayer"; their perspective trivialized as "soft" in a world of "hard" realities.

Within modern industrialist societies, the standing tradition of trivializing, vilifying or pedestalizing mothers seems alive and well. The so-called "Mommy Wars" still rage. A ranking leader in the United States House of Representatives recently implicated "Welfare Moms" in gun violence by seeking to "overmedicate" their children in order to receive additional benefits.[31] Celebrities in every field thank their mothers, and yet of employed single mothers, 63 percent are at the poverty line or below. As Adrienne Rich phrased it, motherhood as "institution" silences the complexity of women's lived realities.[32] Thirty years have passed since she introduced those terms.

We see hints of change, an opening of identities, and yet, the unspoken norm still operates on an exclusive judgment into the "good" and the "not-quite-good-enough." In her introduction to *Twenty-first Century Motherhood: Experience, Identity, Policy, Agency*, Andrea O'Reilly comments how often "the definition of *mother* is [still] limited to heterosexual women who have biological children, while the concept of good motherhood is further restricted to a select group of women who are white, heterosexual, middle-class, able-bodied, married, thirty-something, in a nuclear family with usually one to two children, and ideally, full-time mothers."[33] As Judith Stadtman Tucker points out in one of the essays in this book, "From 'Choice' to Change: Rewriting the Script of Motherhood as Maternal Activism," we need a renewed conversation about how versions of motherhood create an "insurmountable barrier to women's self-actualization and full participation in society."[34]

Forty years after Ikeda first published "Mother," this barrier remains a haunting reality. Becoming a mother remains the largest interrupter of a woman's education, of a woman's mobility, of a woman's earning power, of her health, of the likelihood that she herself will be the primary recipient of healthcare. Quoting Jesse Bernard's groundbreaking work, Tucker reminds her reader that the "terrible hidden underside" to motherhood discussed by Bernard in the 1970s continues to be concealed by the "false aura of romanticism" of the mythic mom, or now Supermom. Tucker shows how the old script persists even in relatively privileged young women who frame a necessitated action as their "own" choice when it was an "accommodation to the scarcity of viable options."[35]

Where then does Ikeda's ideal of "mother" fit? At first, it might seem mired in the old script of "false romanticism." The endless love, the caretaking of small children, the housewife: is this the long-suffering mother who plays a stock part within all hierarchically structured societies? Within such structures, humane versions of mother remain problematic, if not impossible. Hierarchies readily foster unequal power relations. When mixed with firmly demarcated gender roles, the governing societal structures invariably play "mother" (or any societal role) into something that is either "greater than" or "lesser than." To borrow a concept from Ikeda, "harmonized diversity" is not the property of a hierarchically based society.

Here is the greatest challenge posed by Ikeda's mother ideal. Can we devise an approach that reads his poetry from a perspective beyond hierarchies? This is no small task given the fact that each of us has grown up in hierarchical cultures, whether in Japan or the United States. How does one free the mind from the very structures it has unself-consciously adopted? Returning to the 1971 poem "Mother," we see this question played out in the following lines:

> Mother!
> Mothers!
> Never permit the power
> of your gentle love
> to be isolated,
> cut off from others.
> Around a blind, unthinking love
> the shadows of unhappiness
> will gather.
> Only the love
> of compassionate mothers
> linked in solidarity,
> with purpose and reason,
> will set the crucial,
> transforming point of light
> in an otherwise miserable
> and barbaric future.

At first, "gentle" might prove a stumbling block to the reader, evoking images of passivity and insignificance. In my computer's thesaurus, the first word given as a synonym for "gentle" is "mild," which in turn is defined as "slight," "minor," "unimportant." Jettisoning the "standard" definitions, Ikeda identifies "gentle love" with vital power. Himself an advocate of "soft power" (a concept that has recently fallen on hard times given the heightened militarization in our contemporary world), Ikeda equates mothers' power with those who would lead without violence.

Neither can "love" be dismissed as a mistaken ideal in a "real" world. Whose reality, one might ask? Love is certainly a broken ideal in societies maintained through inequity and injustice. If we accept that such societies are the only ones human beings can create, then we agree that love has no lasting societal force. But are these the only possible human societies? Is our own capacity limited to replicating various forms of inequity and injustice? In his 1844 essay "Politics," Emerson pointed out that the true state would be based on love.[36] That essay is not one he is particularly remembered for, though apparently it was one that sounded a resonant note for Martin Luther King Jr.'s understanding of the beloved community.

Consider when Ikeda was writing "Mother," a time in which the voices of and for non-violence were speaking in remarkable cadence throughout the world. As Ikeda points out, this love differs from its stereotyped version as greatly as violence-based societies differ from cultures of peace. In the former, the concept called "love" is exclusive, characterized by different forms of possession. "Blind" and "unthinking," its trustworthiness is questionable. His imagery says this starkly: "shadows of unhappiness" gather around such love. In contrast, Ikeda defines love by the quality of its compassion. As we have seen in his equation of compassion with the sun's radiance, no one is singled out for exclusive attention. In consequence, no one is isolated, cut off or abandoned. In this stanza, he stresses a dynamic of connectedness. Not only are mothers linked to one another in solidarity, but they are linked through "purpose and reason," and their very solidarity itself is defined by those qualities. Informed and active, such alliance enables that operating force of love to be "compassionate" rather than blind.

Here again, contemporary readers may find themselves challenged by the language. In the United States, current associations limit the word "compassion" to a private act between individuals rather than a fundamental value for shaping public policy. Looking at readily available definitions for "good leadership," not one includes "compassion" as an essential quality. If current politicians or CEOs style themselves or are styled as "compassionate," the overwhelming response is distrust. "Compassion" in these cases is seen as a "public-relations cover" for the real actions the leader will undertake. In times of disaster, a leader is allowed compassion for a moment of the nation's attention. But the idea of compassion as a daily, governing principle is almost incomprehensible. When it is interpreted through the existing societal structures, it emerges as either a weak response in a dangerous world or something applicable only to private and individual settings.

In English, the word *compassion* asks the individual to "suffer with" another person. Here again, the reader may wonder about stereotypes returning, because idealizations of "mother" have long celebrated a mother's "suffering." Pegged as the woman who would suffer anything for her children, she bears the brunt of her children's behavior. The real tragedy in this suffering is that it never effects substantive change but seemingly perpetuates an endless cycle where some succeed at another's expense.

Ikeda's poetry once again challenges the reader to move beyond the well-worn narratives. His poems imagine a world where a mother's love would never isolate, exclude or focus on only a few children. Nor would this love be possessive. Nor would it exist at the expense of women. Compassionate love is far different. It is premised on connection, women "linked in solidarity, / with purpose and reason." Imaging mothers as the sun, he offers a narrative that may finally break apart the foundations of the old script. The mother-child bond has long been understood as something profoundly powerful because of its peculiar connection of person-to-person, mother to her *specific* child or children. Whether this has been problematized as the stifling, dominant mother or glorified as the foundation of human stability, that bond has remained essentially unquestioned in mainstream society. The mother loves her children as she loves no other. This love is represented as deeply personal and fiercely attached. It trumps a larger love that recognizes no fundamental distinctions among children.

Now bring back to mind Ikeda's reference to the indiscriminate action of the sun and his extension of that imagery to mothers. The sun radiates: that is its nature. Its life-sustaining properties in no way signify specific attention or attachment. On the sun's part, there is no discrimination. It shines without regard to individuals. Were mothers truly the "sun," the familial attachment in today's definitions of motherhood would be foreign and undesirable. Constraining a mother to such peculiar relations would be like asking the sun to shine sporadically, casting its rays here but not there. By its nature the sun exists without limiting its energy to singular individuals.

Can we envision a world of equitably shared power where relations are modeled by the indiscriminate power of the sun's radiance? That answer remains for the twenty-first century to resolve. In the meantime, I return to the opening words of this essay.

> Become strong!
> Become strong!
> Become strong . . . !

These words resound as the collective poem of women's daily lives. I have heard this poem exchanged among women of all ages and all backgrounds. Often shortened to the definitive, women affirm to one another, "be strong." It translates into every language, and reminds us that poetry matters only when it changes lives.

~

Appreciation runs deep and long. Although written over the course of one short summer, this essay was years in the making. Its very fabric is conversation. Before there were words on the page, there were spoken words circling and circulating among friends. My conversations with Masao Yokota have been invaluable, thought leading to thought and poetry always in the moment. And when Clarissa Douglass joined the conversations, poetry expanded as it always does when compassionate thinkers connect. Conversation, we say, "takes *place*." That phrase is no accident. Even, and perhaps especially, in this era of online chat and e-mail connection, we need real, not virtual, places to converse—to be with one another face to face and difference with difference as together we work with the complexities of understanding.

The Ikeda Center for Peace, Learning, and Dialogue is one such place, fostering a lively home for the imagination where poetry, in the largest sense of that term, thrives. At any time of day, in any part of the world, conversation with Andrew Gebert has been and will always be a dazzling delight. His comments on this essay helped keep doors of possibility open that might all too readily have closed. For my colleagues Ron Bosco and Ken Price, I express ongoing admiration for their work together with enjoyment in all of our exchanges. My extensive and ongoing thanks go to those in Japan who so generously shared their understandings of Daisaku Ikeda's poetry. Those conversations have truly been seeds that will continue to blossom and bear fruit. Clearly those conversations would not have been able to take root had it not been for the untold hours many people spent translating and compiling the poems about which these essays could be written. Not only has theirs been an enormous task given the sheer number of poems but also for the considered attention behind this work. I can only name Yumiko Kato, Andrew Gebert, Richard Walker, Makiko Kuroda, Keiko Kishino and Hans Katayama, offering my ongoing thanks for our fascinating conversation (with lively contributions from Masao Yokota, Richard Yoshimachi and Tetsuo Motoi) about Ikeda's poetry in the context of English-Japanese language differences together with how readers understand their place(s) within the poem. I am deeply grateful to Noriyo A. Sekiyama, Marisa Stenson, Keiko Kakurai and Motoki Kawamorita for their meticulous and thoughtful work in the editing and proofreading stages. Throughout the project, Tetsuo Motoi has effortlessly (it would seem!) answered questions, worked with logistical issues and kept things dynamically structured. He will smile when he reads, "Shall we go now?" And to Patti Voorhis and Cathy Natoli, who kept me sane with mochas, cappuccinos, sometimes just regular coffee *and* more important kept me true to the writing because of our daily conversations, I celebrate friendships that weather every situation.

Notes

1. Translated from Japanese. Daisaku Ikeda, "Become Strong!" (upon receiving an honorary doctorate from the National University of Central Peru on September 4, 1999), *Seikyo Shimbun*, September 5, 1999, p. 2.
2. David Krieger and Daisaku Ikeda, *Choose Hope: Your Role in Waging Peace in the Nuclear Age* (Santa Monica, Calif.: Middleway Press, 2002), p. 153.
3. Audre Lorde, "Poetry is Not a Luxury" in *Sister Outsider: Essays and Speeches* (Freedom, Calif.: The Crossing Press, 1984), p. 37.
4. Ikeda, *Choose Hope*, p. 154.
5. Ibid.
6. Lorde, "Poetry is Not a Luxury" in *Sister Outsider*, p. 37.
7. June Jordan, "For the Sake of People's Poetry: Walt Whitman and the Rest of Us" (1981) in *On Call: Political Essays* (Boston: South End Press, 1985), p. 14.

8. Emily Dickinson, *The Complete Poems of Emily Dickinson*, Thomas H. Johnson, ed. (Boston and Toronto: Little, Brown & Company, 1960), poem #248.
9. Quoted in Heidi Benson, "National Day of Poetry Against the War Today," *San Francisco Chronicle*, February 12, 2003, http://www.commondreams.org/headlines03/0212-02.htm (accessed October 2014). The symposium at the White House had been scheduled for February 12, 2003, but was officially postponed on January 29. In its stead, a number of gatherings around the United States were held under the title "National Day of Poetry Against the War."
10. For further reading, see Mike Chasar, *Everyday Reading: Poetry and Popular Culture in Modern America* (New York: Columbia University Press, 2012), Joan Shelley Rubin, *Songs of Ourselves: The Uses of Poetry in America* (Cambridge, Mass.: Harvard University Press, 2007) and Cary Nelson, *Repression and Recovery: Modern American Poetry and the Politics of Cultural Memory, 1910–1945* (Madison, Wisc.: University of Wisconsin Press, 1989).
11. Ralph Waldo Emerson, *The Collected Works of Ralph Waldo Emerson*, Alfred R. Ferguson, Joseph Slater, Douglas Emory Wilson, Ronald A. Bosco, et al., eds., 10 vols. (Cambridge, Mass., and London: The Belknap Press of Harvard University Press, 1971–2013), 3:10.
12. Muriel Rukeyser, *The Life of Poetry*, Jane Cooper, foreword (Ashfield, Mass.: Paris Press, 1996), Part One: The Resistances, pp. 7–55.
13. Ibid., p. 1.
14. Ibid., p. 15.
15. Ibid., pp. 17–18.
16. Ibid., pp. 10, 11.
17. Ibid., p. 10.
18. Ibid., p. 11.
19. While reader response theory has been applicable to my scholarly work ever since I entered the field, I sadly was never introduced to Rosenblatt's work. In graduate school, we studied Wolfgang Iser. No mention was made of the woman who in the 1930s began publishing her work with actual readers. It was only during this work on Ikeda's poetry and in conversation with good friend and wonderful conversation partner Clarissa Douglass that I learned about Rosenblatt's work. Thanks to Clarissa's wide-ranging reading, she knew Rosenblatt's focus on the interaction of writer, text and reader would interest me.

20. Louise M. Rosenblatt, *Literature as Exploration*, fifth edition, Wayne Booth, foreword (New York: Modern Language Association of America, 1995), p. 23.
21. Louise M. Rosenblatt, "The Poem as Event" in *College English*, 26 (1964): pp. 123–28. Quotation from p. 126.
22. Louise M. Rosenblatt, *The Reader, the Text, the Poem: The Transactional Theory of the Literary Work* (Carbondale and Edwardsville: Southern Illinois University Press, 1978), pp. 20–21.
23. Ibid., pp. 13–14.
24. Rosenblatt, *Literature as Exploration*, pp. 32–33. See also Rosenblatt's discussion of efferent and aesthetic on pp. 292–93.
25. This is really a double quotation. Ikeda's use within the poem refers to Nichiren's "If one lights a fire for others, one will brighten one's own way." (Nichiren, *The Writings of Nichiren Daishonin*, vol. 2, [Tokyo: Soka Gakkai, 2006], p. 1060.)
26. Deserving a study in itself, music is integral to Ikeda's life and work. Not only are musical metaphors prominent in his writings, but he himself is an excellent amateur pianist. During the controversy between the Soka Gakkai and the Nichiren Shoshu priesthood in the late 1970s when Ikeda was under strong pressure from the priesthood not to speak publicly, he turned to the piano for his ongoing poetic expression. He has been instrumental (pun intended) in the vibrant musical groups (choruses, bands) for which the Soka Gakkai is famous. He also founded the Min-On Concert Association, dedicated to the power of peacebuilding through international cultural exchange in the performing arts. It sponsors more than one thousand performances each year, classical to contemporary, traditional to avant-garde. The emphasis is accessibility, so that music, dance, theater can be affordable and so that performers and audiences from different parts of the world may be in creative dialogue with each other. Its name comes from the words *minshu ongaku*, which mean "music for the people." It embodies that name in all of its many dimensions. In Japan, its home is the Min-On Culture Center in Shinjuku Ward, Tokyo, which houses an outstanding circulating music library as well as a listening library, readily available to all. The Culture Center is also home to a music museum that brings together instruments from around the world as well as instruments across time (for example, an exquisite collection of keyboard instruments from a 1580s harpsichord to one of Pablo Casals's pianos).

Composers have set, and continue to set, Ikeda's words to music. Mami Matsubara and Mariko Matsumoto wrote music for a section of "Mother," a piece frequently performed and which I have had the pleasure of hearing on numerous occasions. During a visit to Japan in October 2012, I had the thought-provoking opportunity to speak at length with composer Yoshiko Noda. She described how interactive the composition process can be, with Ikeda weighing in on the character of the music as the piece is being written. The character of the compositions indeed varies with the poems. Her setting for "The people," for example, is a large choral and orchestral work in which the instrumental sections are equally the voice of "the people" with the choral. As she commented in the interview, "I compose because I want to ensure that President Ikeda's poems will be conveyed to future generations. I want to treasure the language. I aim to make the music fit with the language—for it to enhance, as well as be in consonance with the natural rhythms of the language" (Interview, October 5, 2012).

27. As of the writing of this essay, Mr. Hasegawa is Soka Gakkai vice general director; Ms. Kasanuki serves as Soka Gakkai International vice women's leader; and Ms. Maeta, as chairperson of the Soka Gakkai Women's Peace Committee.
28. Conversation with Ms. Kasanuki, October 4, 2012.
29. Adrienne Rich, "What Does a Woman Need to Know" (1979) in *Blood, Bread, and Poetry: Selected Prose, 1979–1985* (New York and London: W. W. Norton & Company, 1986), pp. 5–6.
30. Thus, when Ikeda refers to the Buddhism of the sun, the Japanese reader would immediately be reminded both of Nichiren's name and of the most distinct aspect of Nichiren Buddhism: the Lotus Sutra. Indeed, the phrase "Buddhism of the sun" means Nichiren Buddhism.
31. Rep. Jason Lankford (R-OK) in a meeting with constituents, January 22, 2013, http://www.youtube.com/watch?v=dIops72Xua4 (accessed September 14, 2013).
32. Adrienne Rich, *Of Woman Born: Motherhood as Experience and Institution*, tenth anniversary edition (New York and London: W. W. Norton & Company, 1986) p. 13.
33. Andrea O'Reilly, ed., *Twenty-first Century Motherhood: Experience, Identity, Policy, Agency* (New York: Columbia University Press, 2010), p. 7.
34. Judith Stadtman Tucker, "From 'Choice' to Change: Rewriting the

Script of Motherhood as Maternal Activism," in *Twenty-first Century Motherhood*, p. 301.
35. Ibid., pp. 295, 296, 300.
36. Emerson, *The Collected Works of Ralph Waldo Emerson*, 3:128.

About the Authors

RONALD A. BOSCO is the Distinguished Research Professor of English and American Literature at the University at Albany, SUNY, where he has taught since 1975. An authority on early American literature and, especially, New England Transcendentalism, Bosco recently served as the General Editor of *The Collected Works of Ralph Waldo Emerson* (1971–2013), an edition in ten volumes, for which he oversaw the preparation and publication of the last four volumes, beginning in 2003, and coedited three of them (vols. 7, 8, 10).

KENNETH M. PRICE, Hillegass University Professor of American Literature, codirects the Center for Digital Research at the University of Nebraska–Lincoln. Price recently coedited *Literary Studies in the Digital Age: An Evolving Anthology* (MLA, 2013). His other recent books include *Re-Scripting Walt Whitman* (Blackwell, 2005) and *To Walt Whitman, America* (North Carolina, 2004). Since 1995, Price has codirected *The Walt Whitman Archive*. In 2009, Price received a Digital Innovation Award from the American Council of Learned Societies.

SARAH ANN WIDER is a Professor of English and Women's Studies at Colgate University, Hamilton, New York, where she specializes in the American Renaissance, feminist autobiographical and biographical writings and contemporary Native American literature. Her current studies focus on the women artists and writers of American Transcendentalism. She is former president of the Ralph Waldo Emerson Society and author of *The Critical Reception of Emerson: Unsettling All Things* (Camden House, 2000).

About the Poet

DAISAKU IKEDA was born in Tokyo, Japan, on January 2, 1928, to a family of seaweed farmers. He lived through the devastation of World War II as a teenager and witnessed its senseless horror, which left an indelible mark on his life. His four older brothers were drafted into military service, and the eldest was killed in action. These experiences fueled his lifelong quest and passion to work for peace and people's happiness, rooting out the fundamental causes of human conflict.

In 1947, at the age of nineteen, he met Josei Toda, educator and leader of the Soka Gakkai lay Buddhist society, whose activities are based on the teachings of the thirteenth-century Buddhist reformer Nichiren. Ikeda found Toda to be a man of conviction with a gift for explaining profound Buddhist concepts in logical, accessible terms. Challenging poverty and ill health, he continued his education under the tutelage of Toda, who became his mentor in life.

In May 1960, two years after Toda's death, Ikeda, then thirty-two, succeeded him as president of the Soka Gakkai. He dedicated himself to encouraging the group's members in the process of personal transformation and societal contribution. Under his leadership, the movement began an era of innovation and expansion, fostering individuals committed to the promotion of peace, culture and education. In 1975, Ikeda became the first president of the Soka Gakkai International, now a global network linking some twelve million members in more than 190 countries and territories.

Ikeda is a prolific author of some 100 works ranging from discourses on Buddhism to children's books, poetry and essays. He was named poet laureate by the World Academy of Arts and Culture in 1981. An English-language edition of his poetry, *Journey of Life: Selected Poems of Daisaku Ikeda*, was published by I.B. Tauris in 2014. He is also an avid photographer with a particular love of scenic landscapes and natural beauty. In recognition of his contributions as peacebuilder and educator, Ikeda has been awarded more than 350 academic honors from universities in more than forty countries.